EMPHASIZING DOMINION

AS INTENDED BY GOD

EMPHASIZING DOMINION

AS INTENDED BY GOD

ABINYE D. C. NWANKWO

EMPHASIZING DOMINION

AS INTENDED BY GOD

-Abinye D. C. Nwankwo-

Scripture quotations are taken from different versions of the Holy Bible as indicated.

(KJV) are taken from the King James Version
(NKJV) are taken from the New King James Version
(CEV) are taken from the Contemporary English Version
(GNT) are taken from the Good News Translation.
(AMP) are taken from the Amplified Bible.
(ERV) are taken from the Easy-to-Read Version
(MSG) are taken from the Message Version
(NLT) are taken from the New Living Translation
(BBE) are taken from the Bible in Basic English
(TLB) are taken from The Living Bible
(Darby) are taken from the Darby Version

Independently published

COMMANDING WEALTH

commandingwealth.ng@gmail.com

+2348033805280

ISBN: 979-8-3586-5160-9

DEDICATED TO

All of the gospel preachers who have maintained their commitment to the faith while subduing principalities and powers. Evang. Isobo David-West is one of those people.

ACKNOWLEDGEMENT

I thank God Almighty for the inspiration and grace He gave me while writing this book.

I would especially thank my lovely wife, Dr. Mrs. Mercy Nwankwo. It is indeed a blessing to marry a virtuous woman. She serves as my main editor.

In my Christian journey, Evang. Isobo David-West has been a source of inspiration. His teachings and lifestyle also contributed to the orchestration of Divine concepts for this book. The chronicle of my Christian journey would be incomplete without acknowledging Elder S. N. Solomon and Pastor Oribi Nathan, who carefully sowed the initial seed of God's Word in me.

A special thanks to Prof. Samuel Amaele, who is an excellent encourager. Despite his busy schedule, he proofread and wrote the foreword for this book.

Engr. Abinye D.C. Nwankwo
Children/Teenagers' Ministry
Chapel of the Transfiguration
Ignatius Ajuru University of Education
Port Harcourt.

FOREWORD

Man, by his original nature, is created a champion. He is to have power, authority, and dominion over the earth. Through disobedience (sin) man lost those values. But Jesus Christ restored all, thus bringing man again to his exalted position.

This book of life, written by the anointed man of God, Evangelist Engr. Abinye D. C. Nwankwo, titled "Emphasizing Dominion as Intended by God", is very timely. The very worldly traps that drew man out of the "Golden City", the Garden of Eden, are ever increasing, even in the present generation. Pride, ignorance, greed, unnecessary acquisition of power, among others, have kept men as slaves. What man should command now commands man, and what should have honoured or feared man is now honoured and feared by man. Man of peace now turns to man of wars.

This book of life reminds us of man's redemption, restoration, transfiguration, and transformation. The solution now lies in the Master of the Universe – Jesus Christ; in Him lies the power of dominion. John 1:12

says: "But as many as received Him, to them gave He power to become the sons of God, even to them that believe on His name".

The seven-chaptered book is arranged to save all humanity from self-inflicted injuries, dangers, and damage. It opens up a broad spectrum for human survival and emancipation. It is indeed a book of life and requires and demands that every well-meaning individual, group, association, governmental and non-governmental agencies, and institutions should not only procure, but also study and distribute it to others. It is a must read, study, and apply-book for all Christians.

Evang. Prof. Samuel Amaele (KSC)
Chapel of the Transfiguration
Ignatius Ajuru University of Education
Port Harcourt
Rivers State

PREFACE

During the tenure of one of my chaplains, Rev. Canon Benjamin Orji, we have used the first seven days of the new year for a series of fasting and prayer meetings tagged "Commanding the Year." In the year 2019, he declared the year as that of unlimited Dominion. The chaplain charged me with speaking on '*walking in dominion'* for four sessions of the programme, and by the grace of God, this book was born.

God required someone to exercise dominion over the earth and keep it in shape. It happened that the earth was without form and was empty at one point, and God did not want this to happen again. As a result, the plan for man, which was the purpose of his creation, was for him to have dominion on the drawing board of creation. Following the 'Let Us' conference, man was created.

Man was given the right to have dominion. He was designed to be a replica of God. He started well by giving names to all the animals, and he was operating on an auto-prosperity system. He lost his authority to an imposter as a result of one thing leading to another. Instead of man being 'over' and on top (based on the initial dominion documentation), he came 'under' and beneath. The devil stole man's right.

God, not wanting to abandon His investment, devised a plan to restore man to his original position

Table of Contents

CHAPTER 1

LET THEM HAVE DOMINION

The reason for which something is done or created is its purpose. One of the synonyms for the word "purpose" is "justification". The justification for carrying out a project keeps one on track. When you ask 'Why'; the justification or purpose is the answer to the 'why' question.

Cars are made to be driven: It has been observed that after a car has been driven for a while and later parked in a garage for several months untouched, it may not respond properly when you need to use it after the long period of rest. A telephone is designed for transmitting or receiving calls. Books were published to be read; that makes me happy that you are reading this book. Many people purchase books but do not read them. What is the difference between a person who cannot read and a person who can read but does not? They are likely to be both ignorant. If cars, telephones, books, air-conditioners, wallets, and so on have purposes for which they were made; there also must be a purpose for the creation of man. Young David asked his brother a remarkable question; 'is there not a cause?' Without knowing how the case of David and Goliath ended, we still would have agreed with David that there was a reason for him to be in the battle area; the reason was for him to get food across to his brothers. But we now know that God's ultimate cause was for David to confront Goliath. It is therefore noteworthy that what we perceive as its purpose may not be the ultimate purpose. It is the Creator that knows the ultimate cause, reason, or purpose of a person here on earth at a particular time.

The Image

The online Collins English dictionary defines a ***mirror*** as a "*flat piece of glass which reflects light, so that when you look at it you can see yourself reflected in it. ... If something **mirrors** something else, it has similar features to it, and therefore seems like a copy or representation of it*". The mirror gives an image which could vary in size from the main object; in the case of the side mirror on a vehicle, the image appears smaller than the main object. Representing the object and its reflection with UPPERCASE and lowercase fonts, respectively, we have a CAR and a car (reflection through a mirror). Meditate on this; in the creation event, it became GOD and god.

John 10:34-35(GNT)

Jesus answered, "It is written in your own Law that God said, 'You are gods.' We know that what the Scripture says is true forever; and God called those people gods, the people to whom his message was given.

God is all-powerful. He is the ruler of the universe, the King of kings and the Almighty. He is the Creator of the world. At that point in time, the earth was in a scattered form.

Genesis 1:2 (KJV)

"And the earth was without form, and void; and darkness was upon the face of the deep..."

The "*earth was a soup of nothingness, a bottomless emptiness, an inky blackness*", as the message Bible describes it. Then God worked on and repaired the earth. Thereafter He wanted an image of Him to handle the affairs of things on earth. An image is a reflection, as in a mirror.

Genesis 1:26(MSG)

God spoke: "Let us make human beings in our image, make them reflecting our nature ..."

That was it. Someone may ask if an image can carry power? With unction of understanding, one of the apostles of Jesus demonstrated that images can carry power. It was quite a beautiful sunny day and many folks were coming with their relatives to experience the move of God's power through the hands of the apostles. Then Peter, who towards the end of Jesus' ministry on earth used to be scared, demonstrated something unique;

Acts 5:15-16(KJV)

Insomuch that they brought forth the sick into the streets, and laid them on beds and couches, that at the least the shadow of Peter passing by might overshadow some of them. There came also a multitude out of the cities round about unto Jerusalem, bringing sick folks, and them which were vexed with unclean spirits: and they were healed every one.

According to Dictionary.com, "shadow" is defined as *'a dark figure or* ***image*** *cast on the ground or some* *surface by a body intercepting light*'. The Apostle Peter, most likely for reasons of time and space, dispatched his image (shadow) to work - healing and delivering the oppressed; this incident with Peter demonstrates that an image can carry power. God made man in His own image; man was made to be an express image and exact copy of God's Person (Hebrews 1:3). We began this chapter by discussing justification and purpose. God gives justification for inventing man.

Genesis 1:26(KJV)

And God said, Let us make man in our image, after our likeness: ***and let them have dominion*** *..."*

'Let them have dominion' – This is a mission statement. We were created to have dominion *over the fish of the sea, and over the fowl of the air, and over the cattle, and over all the earth, and over every creeping thing that creepeth upon the earth.* I mentioned earlier that the justification for carrying out a project helps one to be on track. God has always kept track and focus on man because of this purpose. Hence He has been so mindful of man.

Psalms 8:4,6(KJV)

What is man, that thou art mindful of him? and the son of man, that thou visitest him? Thou madest him to have dominion over the works of thy hands; thou hast put all things under his feet:

Authority

During the events of Genesis 1, the devil was already on earth. God then needed someone to coordinate things on earth. Bring to mind the Sunday School lessons; that Lucifer attempted a coup d'état along with one-third of the angels in heaven;

Ezekiel 28:14-15 (KJV)

Thou art the anointed cherub that covereth; and I have set thee so: thou wast upon the holy mountain of God; thou hast walked up and down in the midst of the stones of fire. Thou wast perfect in thy ways from the day that thou wast created, till iniquity was found in thee.

Isaiah 14:12-14 (KJV)

How art thou fallen from heaven, O Lucifer, son of the morning! how art thou cut down to the ground, which didst weaken the nations! For thou hast said in thine heart, I will ascend into heaven, I will exalt my throne above the stars of God: I will sit also upon the mount of the congregation, in the sides of the north: I will ascend above the heights of the clouds; I will be like the most High.

Revelation 12:7-9(KJV)

And there was war in heaven: Michael and his angels fought against the dragon; and the dragon fought and his angels, And prevailed not; neither was their place found any more in heaven. And the great dragon was cast out, that old serpent, called the Devil, and Satan, which deceiveth the whole world: he was cast out into the earth, and his angels were cast out with him.

The devil was thrown down after the coup attempt. Hence the devil's base changed. God Almighty decided to show forth his supremacy over the devil. It was like God saying, 'I do not need to deal with the devil myself, let a lesser me (god) deal with him to belittle him.

Consider the following skit to explain the word 'belittle'. A professor had a driver who had worked with him for a long time. The driver usually goes with the professor for most of his presentations; so much so that he could even present articles like the professor. On a fateful day, a two-hour presentation was scheduled; the professor was quite tired and opted to cancel it. At that moment, the driver told the professor that he could handle it since he had listened to that same presentation several times. They came to an agreement that the driver would dress like the professor while the boss would do the work of the driver and sit in the audience. The scheduled time arrived, and the presentation was excellently handled; it was then time for questions, and a highly ranked lecturer asked a highly technical question. It was actually difficult for the driver to answer, but as smart as he was, he 'belittled' the high-ranked lecturer by saying, 'what a cheap question which even my driver can answer'. And he called his 'driver' (the actual professor) who gave an excellent response.

Genesis 1:26(KJV)

And God said, Let us make man in our image, after our likeness: ***and let them have dominion*** *..."*

Psalms 8:6 (KJV)

Thou madest him to have dominion over the works of thy hands; ***thou hast put all things under his feet****:*

God's intention for man was demonstrated by the 'second Adam'. According to 1 Corinthians 15:45–47, Jesus is referred to as the second Adam. Jesus, hence, demonstrated the belittling purpose that God had concerning the devil.

Colossians 2:15(GNT)

" ... he made a public spectacle of them by leading them as captives in his victory procession".

Jesus made a public spectacle of the devil. In other words, he belittled and rubbished the devil. Being the second Adam, he was to be an example of what man was created for.

1 John 3:8(KJV)

"... For this purpose the Son of God was manifested, that he might destroy the works of the devil."

There are matters we ought to handle ourselves, but we keep bringing God down. Do you remember the song, 'Oh Lord, come down and manifest your power'? In many countries, you have a president and, under him, governors. There are areas in which the governors are to exercise dominion. So God made man and said, 'Let them have dominion'. Knowing his rights, Elijah could by his own word command rain to hold its peace. See the final section of 1 Kings 17:1 in two translations.

"... there shall not be dew nor rain these years, but according to my word." (KJV)

"... I tell you that there will be no dew or rain for the next two or three years until I say so." (GNT)

A man's account was documented several years ago; witches met and decided to hold their world conference in Africa, specifically in Benin, Nigeria. Their chief host held a press conference and proudly announced to the media that Benin City would host the first universal conference of witches and wizards. Dr. Benson Idahosa, of blessed memory, stated that it was NOT possible. 'If I am a man of God!' he exclaimed. It couldn't be true, it couldn't be possible!' The press inquired as to what he would do if they came. 'I would kill them all,' he replied. When informed of Idahosa's statement, the proposed chief host responded, "Not even God can stop it." The press rushed to the man of God, claiming that the chief host had stated that not even God could stop it. Dr. Benson Idahosa simply agreed with the chief host. "What?" the shocked press asked. Idahosa told them that God did not need to waste time preventing witches from attending a conference in Benin-City. "That is why I am here. The Lord does not need to think about trivial matters like stopping the witches' conference." Idahosa could handle it on his own, and the proposed conference did not take place. That was a man wielding power and exercising dominion. That was authority.

CHAPTER 2

DOMINION AS A RIGHT

The word translated as dominion in Genesis 1:26 is from the Hebrew word 'radah'. The word, radah, which appears about 27 times in the Old Testament has been translated at different points in the King James Version as dominate, rule, and reign. It is a word that involves authority. Dominion is therefore a right of governance. The devil understands what dominion means, so he goes around thriving on man's ignorance.

Let us make man... and let them have dominion. God had a discussion as portrayed in the first chapter of Genesis. It was, there, agreed that man be given the right or authorisation for dominion. On the other hand, the devil was longing to have dominion.

The Stomach Issue

A social proverb goes, 'the way to a man's heart is through his stomach.' My intention is not to start a debate about the proverb but to show how the devil works to bring man down. Daniel made his decision because he did not want to gamble with his destiny as a young man.

Daniel 1:8(KJV)

But Daniel purposed in his heart that he would not defile himself with the portion of the king's meat, nor with the wine which he drank: therefore he requested of the prince of the eunuchs that he might not defile himself.

The "stomach," which represents the desire to satisfy the flesh, is one strategic area where the devil seeks to tempt man. It falls under the category of "lust of the flesh," as depicted in 1 John 2:15-17. Let us meditate on that Scripture;

1 John 2:15-17(KJV)

Love not the world, neither the things that are in the world. If any man love the world, the love of the Father is not in him. For all that is in the world, the lust of the flesh, and the lust of the eyes, and the pride of life, is not of the Father, but is of the world. And the world passeth away, and the lust thereof: but he that doeth the will of God abideth for ever.

Genesis 1:26(KJV)

*And God said, Let us make **man** in our image, after our likeness: and let **them** have dominion...*

God created man, male and female He created them. Hence, in the next few pages, when I mention the first 'man'– I am referring to the first 'them'. While the second Adam refers to Jesus as mentioned in chapter one based on the Scriptures.

The devil kept looking for an avenue to get the password for dominion. In computer technology; if someone gets hold of your password, he gets access to everything that password was intended to unlock. The intriguing but dangerous aspect of using a password carelessly is that the adversary can enter the system, manipulate it, and lock out the original owner.

The lust of the flesh or the stomach is a ready avenue where rights are exchanged. This path has been taken several times in Scripture, most notably by Judas Iscariot, who betrayed his master out of greed. You know, the devil is very tricky; he made Judas believe that after getting the money, Jesus would escape. Judas had witnessed Jesus escaping in previous times;

Luke 4:29 -30(GNT)

They rose up, dragged Jesus out of town, and took him to the top of the hill on which their town was built. They meant to throw him over the cliff, but he walked through the middle of the crowd and went his way.

Master Escaper Season 1; what he did before, he can do it again. Judas would have assumed that the contract was only to identify Jesus, so a prison break would not be considered a breach of contract. Several ladies have destroyed their destinies as a result of the Stomach issue. Several years ago, I was in Kaduna State, Nigeria, when there was a knock at the door. I was not expecting anyone, but when I opened the door, a young girl walked in. She needed money, so she asked that I have sex with her and give her money. She was probably a recruit in that line. What age are you? I was curious. She was seventeen at the time (just a teenager). I asked her, 'Are you not bothered about getting pregnant?'. Her response revealed the devil's trick; she said I could get a condom but if it was not available, she had done her calculations so she would not conceive. These are tricks the devil brings into the path of our teenagers to destroy them. One Sunday after worship, a young girl approached me, moved by the preacher's message. She sobbed as she told me how she had defiled herself with a boy who was supposed to help her with her Senior Secondary Certificate exam. She came seeking assurance of God's forgiveness. Teenagers today are suffering greatly as a result of the devil's tricks through the lust of the flesh. For the seventeen-year-old girl, she realized after some discussion that she was treading on dangerous ground.

Another example is that of Esau and Jacob. Esau was the first son of Isaac and hence had a right or authority called the birthright. Esau, however, despised his right. It is the "Esau" syndrome that makes people sell their conscience and future for some community or political relevance. There are innocent-looking people who have joined occult societies for the sake of jobs. There comes a time when they want their freedom to marry or conceive and would not succeed. Go through Esau's case with the message Bible;

Hebrews 12:16-17(MSG)

Watch out for the Esau syndrome: trading away God's lifelong gift in order to satisfy a short-term appetite. You well know how Esau later regretted that impulsive act and wanted God's blessing—but by then it was too late, tears or no tears.

Some people destroy their future for instant gratification. Do not sell your right; you may just be close to your breakthrough.

Genesis 25:29-34(KJV)

And Jacob sod pottage: and Esau came from the field, and he was faint: And Esau said to Jacob, Feed me, I pray thee, with that same red pottage; for I am faint: therefore was his name called Edom. And Jacob said, Sell me this day thy birthright. And Esau said, Behold, I am at the point to die: and what profit shall this birthright do to me? And Jacob said, Swear to me this day; and he sware unto him: and he sold his birthright unto Jacob. Then Jacob gave Esau bread and pottage of lentiles; and he did eat and drink, and rose up, and went his way: thus Esau despised his birthright.

To Esau, it was just a mere talk to say that Jacob could have the birthright. According to Genesis 25:34, he ate, drank, rose up, and went on his way as if nothing happened. The devil makes one feel that a decision is merely inconsequential. People have joined cult groups by just filling out a form and feeling that since there was no blood covenant, it had no effect on them. The phrase 'it doesn't matter' has destroyed several destinies. Esau fell for the stomach issue.

The devil continued to seek a way to bring man beneath him. It is written that the devil moves to and fro, seeking whom to destroy. He kept looking for loopholes and any legal means to take hold of power.

Romans 6:16(KJV)

Know ye not, that to whom ye yield yourselves servants to obey, his servants ye are to whom ye obey; whether of sin unto death, or of obedience unto righteousness?

That appears to be the principle required by the devil to achieve his goal, that 'you are the slaves of him whom you obey'. That means that if the devil can make a man obey him, then he rises above the man. The devil immediately went to work on his idea. What the devil seeks to achieve in any temptation is for the victim to obey him. The devil used the same strategy for the first and second Adam.

Genesis 3:4-6(KJV)

And the serpent said unto the woman, Ye shall not surely die: For God doth know that in the day ye eat thereof, then your eyes shall be opened, and ye shall be as gods, knowing good and evil. <u>And when the woman saw that the tree was good for food</u>, and that it was pleasant to the eyes, and a tree to be desired to make one wise, <u>she took of the fruit thereof, and did eat</u>, and gave also unto her husband with her; and he did eat.

The devil talked till the tree was seen to be good for food. It became a stomach issue. It is written in Ephesians 4:27, 'neither give place to the devil'. Several people fall for tricks when they keep listening to deceivers. Give the devil an inch and he will go a mile. He tried same trick on Jesus (the second Adam) when he asked Jesus to turn stone into bread so that it would be good for food. In that case, however, Jesus did not give place to the devil.

When the first Adam ate from the tree which God said should not be eaten, he completed the circuit for the devil to act. "Know ye not, that to whom ye yield yourselves servants to obey, his servants ye are to whom ye obey". The man obeyed the devil, and that turned the table. The devil became the god of this world. In Genesis 3:5, the devil promised 'man' that they would be as gods if they ate from the tree; but it was he (the devil) that became the god. Many people or firms will present you with seemingly wonderful business proposals, promising that you will become wealthy; however, by the time you are involved, they will be the ones who have become wealthy, not you. Be wise.

It became a day that the adversary, the devil, was happy. He had assumed a high position because his status had changed. Man came under the influence of satanic forces. God would occasionally place His Spirit on men who would shake the demonic kingdom. Men like Sampson would carry a city gate up a hill when the Spirit comes on him; Elijah would call down fire and kill satanic priests.

It was then time for God to start a process to redeem man. He needed a man. In the beginning He created or invented man. He did not have to reinvent the wheel;

since there is already a system in place for man to be born. So He had to put his Spirit into a virgin to bring forth the Man. The Man, Adam; I mean the second Adam was born. He was named Jesus. Shepherds came to celebrate His birth, and wise men from far and wide brought gifts, but Herod, the king at the time, attempted to kill him. The second Adam was born so that He would die the death of redemption but, as a Child, it was not time to die. Hence, God planned his escape from Herod. For the second Adam needed to grow to the size of the first Adam to replay the 'match'.

Luke 1:80(KJV)

And the child grew, and waxed strong in spirit, and was in the deserts till the day of his shewing unto Israel.

Jesus had just finished a forty days fasting and prayer session. The devil was set to replay the match he had with the first Adam. It was a contest of who will obey.

Matthew 4:2-4(KJV)

And when he had fasted forty days and forty nights, he was afterward an hungred. And when the tempter came to him, he said, If thou be the Son of God, command that these stones be made bread. But he answered and said, It is written, Man shall not live by bread alone, but by every word that proceedeth out of the mouth of God.

Most of the time, satan will tempt you based on your needs. He recognised Jesus' hunger and remembered the stomach issue, so he said, "Command that these stones be made bread." Remember, it was a contest to see who would obey. 'It is written,...' said Jesus in response.

"Mr. Second Adam," the devil reasoned, "you are not the only one who knows what is written." So the devil had him stand on the temple's highest point. The devil then told Jesus,

Matthew 4:6-7(KJV)
... If thou be the Son of God, cast thyself down: ***for it is written,*** *He shall give his angels charge concerning thee: and in their hands they shall bear thee up, lest at any time thou dash thy foot against a stone. Jesus said unto him, It is written again, Thou shalt not tempt the Lord thy God.*

The match was getting tough. In the first match, it was just one blow and the man fell. What is happening?

The devil understood that this second Adam really wanted to gain back the dominion, the kingdom, and the glory. With the same kind of trick in which he got the first man, he suggested to Jesus that instead of going through much stress, he could hand over the dominion only if Jesus would just bow down. The idea was that if Jesus obeys, the game ends and he (the devil) retains the dominion. Similar to when Adam obeyed him to be as god, only for the devil to be the god.

Matthew 4:8-9(KJV)

Again, the devil taketh him up into an exceeding high mountain, and sheweth him all the kingdoms of the world, and the glory of them; And saith unto him, All these things will I give thee, if thou wilt fall down and worship me.

Let us look at the response of Jesus using the Good News Bible

Matthew 4:10-11(GNT)

*Then Jesus answered, "**Go away, Satan**! The Scripture says, 'Worship the Lord your God and serve only him!' "* ***Then the Devil left*** *Jesus; and angels came and helped him.*

Jesus commanded Satan to go away and Satan left. Who obeyed? Match ended. I like the song that says, 'Obey oh, Obey oh, Obey: Satan must obey Jesus, Obey'

It was a technical knockout. For this purpose the Son of God was manifested, that he might destroy the works of the devil (1 John 3:8). *And* having spoiled principalities and powers, he made a show of them openly, triumphing over them in it (Colossians 2:15). Hallelujah.

CHAPTER 3

WALKING IN DOMINION

Dominion means sovereignty or control. God Almighty is Sovereign and in control. You cannot be like Him and still not be like Him. It would be an aberration for a lion to give birth to a goat and gross anomaly for an orange tree to bring forth pineapple fruit. God's plan was for man to have dominion.

Genesis 1:26(KJV)

And God said, Let us make man in our image, after our likeness: and let them have dominion <u>over</u> the fish of the sea, and <u>over</u> the fowl of the air, and <u>over</u> the cattle, and <u>over</u> all the earth, and <u>over</u> every creeping thing that creepeth upon the earth.

God said, '*...and let them have dominion over...*'. An online Dictionary defines the preposition 'over' to mean '*at a higher level or layer than*', it can also mean being above. God's plan for man was for him to be at the helm of affairs. It is usually said that getting success is not as difficult as maintaining it. It is actually debatable anyway. God placed man at the top and it was man's responsibility to remain and maintain the position.

Deuteronomy 28:13(KJV)

> *And the LORD shall make thee the head, and not the tail; and thou shalt be above only, and thou shalt not be beneath;...*

If you look through legal documents or rules and regulations, you are likely to come across the verb 'shall' several times. The verb, 'shall', could refer to legal duty or formal instruction, though sometimes it could express a future tense. The passage in Deuteronomy 28:13 expresses the fact that God makes you the head and takes you to the top, while you have the responsibility to (you shall) remain above. The temptation you face is not an excuse to fail, for it is written *"Oh Man, thou art inexcusable"*. How come, when a person is caught in a crime, then it was the devil that pushed him? It is written '*resist the devil and he will flee from you*'.

1 Corinthians 10:13(KJV)

There hath no temptation taken you but such as is common to man: but God is faithful, who will not suffer you to be tempted above that ye are able; but will with the temptation also make a way to escape, that ye may be able to bear it.

That temptation is not beyond your limit. You have a responsibility. You shall remain above only. Stay up! Do not fall for that immoral act. You can escape as Joseph did, in Genesis chapter 39. He escaped despite intense pressure. God made us to have dominion; we therefore have the responsibility to walk in dominion.

The Authority for Dominion

Definition of authority (according to Oxford dictionary) - the power or right to give orders, make decisions, and enforce obedience.

Definition of authority (according to Cambridge dictionary) - the moral or legal right to control.

There are things we do in Church which we do not have the moral standing to do. We see people who are promiscuous teaching marriage seminars; people who are like Judas Iscariot teaching financial principles. There are folks in the choir who are as disobedient as an undisciplined mind singing 'Trust and Obey' in church; folks whose body is far from the altar singing 'I surrender all'. A pathetic example is recorded in the book of Acts ;

Acts 19:11-16(KJV)

And God wrought special miracles by the hands of Paul: So that from his body were brought unto the sick handkerchiefs or aprons, and the diseases departed from them, and the evil spirits went out of them. Then certain of the vagabond Jews, exorcists, took upon them to call over them which had evil spirits the name of the Lord Jesus, saying, We adjure you by Jesus whom Paul preacheth. And there were seven sons of one Sceva, a Jew, and chief of the priests, which did so. And the evil spirit answered and said, Jesus I know, and Paul I know; but who are ye? And the man in whom the evil spirit was leaped on them, and overcame them, and prevailed against them, so that they fled out of that house naked and wounded.

'*God wrought special miracles by the hands of Paul*'; it points to the fact that Paul had received the authority or rights to use the key. Consider a house setting; the children have authority to go to different rooms in the house. When they get to a locked room, they use the key to open the door. For a stranger does not have the right to enter the house, so if found with the keys, it means the keys were stolen. In Acts 19:13,14, certain vagabonds, the seven sons of Sceva, tried to open the room of deliverance with the key (the name of Jesus) without the necessary authority. In a dramatic simulation, an evil spirit looked at the seven men and said something like, 'On the database for authorization, I see names like Jesus and even Paul but your names are not there' and the man in whom the evil spirit was, leaped on them and overcame them, and prevailed against them, so that they fled out of that house naked and wounded.

When you possess authority, even your steps are different. Some law enforcement agents are able to detect criminals by looking at their eyes and steps. When you have and understand authority, your confidence is enhanced. People were able to differentiate between the teachings of Jesus and the Scribes.

Matthew 7:28-29(KJV)

And it came to pass, when Jesus had ended these sayings, the people were astonished at his doctrine: For he taught them as one having authority, and not as the scribes.

Mark 1:27(KJV)

And they were all amazed, insomuch that they questioned among themselves, saying, What thing is this? what new doctrine is this? for with authority commandeth he even the unclean spirits, and they do obey him.

With authority, Jesus commanded devils and they obeyed him. Jesus was a custodian of such authority. The disciples were privileged, in that Jesus gave them this authority.

Luke 9:1(KJV)

Then he called his twelve disciples together, and gave them power and authority over all devils, and to cure diseases.

The Keys of the Kingdom

The implication of an earlier explanation is that a child may have the authority and can go anywhere in the house, but if he does not have the keys he would be limited. Hence the disciple needed and got the keys.

Matthew 16:19(KJV)

And I will give unto thee the keys of the kingdom of heaven: and whatsoever thou shalt bind on earth shall be bound in heaven: and whatsoever thou shalt loose on earth shall be loosed in heaven.

The kingdom has keys (plural) for different doors. There is the key of David as described in Isaiah 22:22 and Revelations 3:7, also the key of knowledge was mentioned in Luke 11:52.

Isaiah 22:22(KJV)

And the key of the house of David will I lay upon his shoulder; so he shall open, and none shall shut; and he shall shut, and none shall open.

Revelation 3:7(KJV)

And to the angel of the church in Philadelphia write; These things saith he that is holy, he that is true, he that hath the key of David, he that openeth, and no man shutteth; and shutteth, and no man openeth;

Luke 11:52(KJV)

Woe unto you, lawyers! for ye have taken away the key of knowledge: ye entered not in yourselves, and them that were entering in ye hindered.

I went with my family to Bayelsa State in Nigeria towards the end of the year 2018. We wanted the children to stay with their grannies during the festive holidays. When we arrived in our vehicle, desiring to enter the gate, the gate was locked. Luckily, my sister-in-law came with a bunch of keys in order to open the gate. We waited for a while. She tried her best to open the gate, but to no avail. She advised us to park outside the gate because, from the bunch containing many keys, she was not sure which one was for the gate. She kept trying different ones until she was somewhat frustrated. Do you remember quadratic equations from your math classes? Not knowing which method would produce the answer the quickest: factorization, square roots, completing the square, or graph method.

In Matthew 16:19, Jesus introduces the keys of the kingdom to the disciples. Exactly a chapter later, in Matthew 17:19, the disciples called Jesus to one side and questioned him concerning the bunch of keys they had received and how they could not open a particular door. Jesus looked at them and explained to them that Faith as a key can open doors, but this particular door, however, needed a different key still in the bunch. As a playwright, I tried to dramatize it in this paragraph, but let us look at it as presented in Scripture.

Matthew 17:19-21 (KJV)

Then came the disciples to Jesus apart, and said, Why could not we cast him out? And Jesus said unto them, Because of your unbelief: for verily I say unto you, If ye have faith as a grain of mustard seed, ye shall say unto this mountain, Remove hence to yonder place; and it shall remove; and nothing shall be impossible unto you. Howbeit <u>this kind goeth not out but by prayer and fasting</u>.

God has given us all we need to walk in dominion. Take the step. If we claim to be joint heirs with Christ, we must walk in dominion as He did.

1 John 2:6(KJV)

He that saith he abideth in him ought himself also so to walk, even as he walked.

CHAPTER 4

KEYS FOR DOMINION

It has been established that the Kingdom of God operates by keys. When God said, 'let them have dominion', He meant what He said. Hence He is ever ready to support you in fulfilling the dominion mandate. For it is He that works in you both to will and do of His good pleasure. Here are some keys to dominion;

1. Knowing your right

The story was told of a young man who had longed to go on a journey in a ship. It took him several months to be able to save the transport fare. He made his plan to survive through the journey because he had no more money to afford the expensive food through the journey of several days. Whenever it was time for food, he would make an excuse to go to the toilet. It continued for days. On the last day of the trip, an observant person called him aside and asked why he had not been joining others for breakfast, lunch, and dinner. Moreover, he appeared lean. It was then that the young man opened up that he had used his last savings to pay for the trip and had no extra funds to afford the meals. So at meal times, he went out to eat part of the biscuits he brought along. The friend told him that the fare paid covered all the meals throughout the journey. You can imagine the regrets. That last day, when he appeared at the meal stand and started eating, everyone knew someone had visited.

When you are unaware of your rights, you can be greatly limited. In every facet of life, you need to know your rights and entitlements. If not, you may be cheated. Do you know that you are a member of God's family?

Ephesians 1:5(CEV)

God was kind and decided that Christ would choose us to be God's own adopted children.

Galatians 4:6-7(CEV)

Now that we are his children, God has sent the Spirit of his Son into our hearts. And his Spirit tells us that God is our Father. You are no longer slaves. You are God's children, and you will be given what he has promised.

Therefore if you are in Christ, you are one of the adopted children of God with full rights. What is available to you as a member of His family?

Romans 8:17(KJV)

And if children, then heirs; heirs of God, and joint-heirs with Christ; if so be that we suffer with him, that we may be also glorified together.

Being joint-heir with Christ implies that we can access what Christ can access. You need to know what accessories God has provided for you and leave the ones He did not provide. It is clearly stated in Scripture that God did not provide 'fear' to you, so do not operate with that tool.

2Timothy 1:7(KJV)

For God hath not given us the spirit of fear; but of power, and of love, and of a sound mind.

I tell people that if you see the spirit of fear operating in one's life; it was not God that gave it. It is either the person picked it from somewhere or stole it. There are people who keep forwarding messages, such as the one that claims that if you pick up a call from a particular phone number, you will die. That is nonsense to a person who knows his rights in Christ. Some social media texts will compel you to forward a message to ten people within twenty-four hours or bad luck will surface. And a believer who might have stolen the spirit of fear from somewhere would start forwarding to twenty people in twelve hours; that is an error.

Jesus did not operate by the spirit of fear. God did not give you the spirit of fear, but according to 2 Timothy 1:7, He gave you power of sonship as reiterated in John 1:12;

John 1:12(KJV)

But as many as received him, to them gave he power to become the sons of God, even to them that believe on his name

You have therefore received power to be called a son of God. Also he gave us by His love

1 John 3:1(KJV)

Behold, what manner of love the Father hath bestowed upon us, that we should be called the sons of God: therefore the world knoweth us not, because it knew him not.

Note that some dreams are a ploy of the devil to get access into one's life through fear. I heard the story of a man who had a dream one calm night. Before that, he had been experiencing hardship. In the dream, he saw a masquerade chasing after him. He ran with all the strength he could muster, but unfortunately, he tripped. The masquerade caught up with him and brought out a big sword. Without delay, the masquerade cut off his head and he woke up. Instead of allowing fear to take hold of him, he started dancing and rejoicing. Why is he rejoicing instead of crying? He changed the narrative. He said that it was the evil things that had been disturbing him that were cut off. That was how the change in his life came. He started prospering.

The devil thrives where believers drive in ignorance. 2 Corinthians 2:11 makes it clear that if we are ignorant of his devices, Satan would take advantage of us.

Sometimes it takes knowledge to gain deliverance. Jesus said in Matthew 9:12 ' They that be whole need not a physician, but they that are sick'. In other words, those who need a doctor are they who are sick, and *those who need deliverance are they who are in captivity*. I was once in a particular church's WhatsApp group, when a seeming over-zealous pastor's 'commandant' almost called down angels to shut me up for mentioning in the group that believers could be in need of deliverance. It was God who made a profound statement in the following Scripture;

Isaiah 5:13(KJV)

Therefore my people are gone into captivity, because they have no knowledge: and their honourable men are famished, and their multitude dried up with thirst.

Those in captivity are candidates for deliverance. And God saying 'my people' means believers. It is usually said that knowledge is power. Knowing your right to dominion keeps you on top. There are people who are in captivity health-wise, financially and in several areas, because *they have* no knowledge. Beloved, know your rights as a joint-heir with Christ.

Properly align your thoughts

A quote attributed to Joyce Meyer reads, 'You cannot have a positive life and a negative mind' at the same time. Indeed, you are a reflection of your thoughts.

When a person thinks how tiring a job can be, the organs in his body tend to discuss this amongst themselves, saying, 'Our boss says we are tired on this job, so let us all comply and be tired'.

I read through an interesting story credited to Bruno Klopfer in 1957; a doctor was handling the medical case of Mr. Wright, who had an advanced cancer. All treatments had failed, and time was running out. The doctor did not expect him to last a week.

Mr. Wright desperately wanted to live, and he heard of a promising new drug called Krebiozen. He believed the drug would be his miracle cure, and kept disturbing the doctor to administer it to him. The medical practitioner reluctantly injected him with Krebiozen.

Surprisingly, a few days later, the patient was up and walking around. About ten days later, he left the hospital, allegedly cancer free.

Mr. Wright kept praising Krebiozen as a miracle drug for two months until a scientific report showed that Krebiozen was not an effective drug for cancer. Mr.

Wright, who believed the scientific report, fell into despair, and his cancer returned.

This time, the doctor, who genuinely wanted to save the patient, decided to play a fast one, thereby lying that some of the initial supplies of the drug deteriorated during shipping, making them less effective, but that he had gotten a new batch of highly concentrated Krebiozen, which he could give him.

The doctor then injected Mr. Wright with nothing but distilled water. And a seemingly miraculous thing happened – again. Mr. Wright was feeling great again for another two months.

Then the American Medical Association blew it by announcing that a nationwide study of Krebiozen proved that the drug was utterly worthless. This time, Mr. Wright lost all faith in his treatment. His cancer came right back, and he died two days later.

Proverbs 23:7(KJV)
For as he thinketh in his heart, so is he:

The limitations you experienced last year could be based on your mentality. If there is a change in how you think, there will be a change in what happens around you. The mentality effect does not affect only individuals, it affects organisations. For instance, you may have company A permitting its staff to go by first class ticket on a flight for a course, and company B feels it should always save cost, therefore insists on its staff going by road on the same journey. Ordinarily, one might expect company B to be very prosperous since it is saving a lot, but the reverse would very often be the case.

Proverb 11:24(KJV)

There is that scattereth, and yet increaseth; and there is that withholdeth more than is meet, but it tendeth to poverty.

I have seen Churches with similar mind-sets having similar results, while some others who are only good at criticising and condemning success being nowhere. It is difficult to put someone with a winning mentality down; it is like trying to put an inflated balloon under water.

You tend to become what you think of yourself. Some spies, as recorded in the Book of Numbers, said that "we were in our own sight as grasshoppers, and so we were in their sight".

Numbers 13:25-27(Darby)

And they returned from searching out the land after forty days.

And they came, and went to Moses and to Aaron, and to the whole assembly of the children of Israel, to the wilderness of Paran, to Kadesh; and brought back word to them, and to the whole assembly; and shewed them the fruit of the land.

And they told him, and said, We came to the land to which thou didst send us, and surely it floweth with milk and honey; and this is the fruit of it.

Moses sent out spies into the land of Jericho, and all of them saw the same thing, which was that the land **surely flowed with milk and honey.** Yet their mentality differentiated them.

Numbers 13:30 - 33(GNT)

Caleb silenced the people who were complaining against Moses, and said, "We should attack now and take the land; we are strong enough to conquer it." But the men who had gone with Caleb said, "No, we are not strong enough to attack them; the people there are more powerful than we are." So they spread a false report among the Israelites about the land they had explored. They said, "That land doesn't even produce enough to feed the people who live there. Everyone we saw was very tall, and we even saw giants there, the descendants of Anak. We felt as small as grasshoppers, and that is how we must have looked to them."

I cannot tell you that Caleb's version was the most accurate compared to the other spies. He only told Moses how he felt, his thoughts and mind-set. It may be difficult to deny that there are some occultic forces in your village, but what is your mind-set over them, is it that of dominion over them? Forty-five years later, Caleb recalled his report...

Joshua 14:7(ERV)

Moses, the LORD'S servant, sent me to look at the land where we were going. I was 40 years old at that time. When I came back, I told Moses <u>what I thought</u> about the land.

Caleb did not deny that there were giants (the Anakites) in the land, but he was resolute that 'we are strong enough to conquer'. The others kept seeing themselves as grasshoppers. There are many students who are failing hopelessly because the see themselves as grasshoppers in the midst of other seemingly good students. A point in time in my secondary school days, I was recklessly poor in mathematics. I was later taken to another school where I expected that the students I was going to meet were internationally configured in mathematics. Despite this, I refused to see myself as a grasshopper and instead worked to become the top math student in my class and meritoriously had the highest grade in Mathematics during my Senior Secondary Certificate Examination.

There are people who consider themselves spent and unable to improve after the age of sixty, but not Caleb. He aligned his thoughts properly; his mentality did not change even at age eighty-five.

Joshua 14:6 - 12(MSG)

The people of Judah came to Joshua at Gilgal. Caleb son of Jephunneh the Kenizzite spoke: "You'll remember what GOD said to Moses the man of God concerning you and me back at Kadesh Barnea.

I was forty years old when Moses the servant of GOD sent me from Kadesh Barnea to spy out the land. And I brought back an honest and accurate report.

My companions who went with me discouraged the people, but I stuck to my guns, totally with GOD, my God.

That was the day that Moses solemnly promised, 'The land on which your feet have walked will be your inheritance, you and your children's, forever. Yes, you have lived totally for GOD.'

Now look at me: GOD has kept me alive, as he promised. It is now forty-five years since GOD spoke this word to Moses, years in which Israel wandered in the wilderness. <u>And here I am today, eighty-five years old! I'm as strong as I was the day Moses sent me out. I'm as strong as ever in battle, whether coming or going.</u> So give me this hill country that GOD promised me. You yourself heard the report, that the Anakim were there with their great fortress cities. If GOD goes with me, I will drive them out, just as GOD said."

Thoughts can either make or defile your destiny. When Jesus gave a list of items that can defile and destroy man, thought was top on it. Note that thoughts can be good or evil. Evil thoughts are the ones that defile and make you to be under the devil's influence. The scribes and Pharisees came to Jesus to query his disciple's propensity for neglecting tradition; for the disciples were eating with unwashed hands. Jesus replied, 'Not what enters into the mouth defiles the man; but what goes forth out of the mouth, this defiles the man.'

Jesus went further to tell us what he meant, 'Out of the abundance of the heart, the mouth speaks'. He then gave a list of items from the heart that defiles. Behold the list;

Matthew 15:19 *For out of the heart come forth*
;

- *evil thoughts,*
- *murders,*
- *adulteries,*
- *fornications,*
- *thefts,*
- *false witnessings,*
- *blasphemies;*

Matthew 15:20a *these are the things which defile man; (Darby)*

The first thing on the list is 'evil thoughts'. Thoughts could show up as an imagination, which is the formation of an image in one's mind. No wonder Paul wrote in 2 Corinthians 10:5 *'Casting down imaginations... and bringing every thought into captivity to the obedience of Christ'*. I had earlier shown that an image can carry power; which implies that some images formed in your mind as imaginations are powerful. The image can pull you down if you do not respond fast enough, hence casting down imaginations.

2. Hold on to God's Word

One man who literally walked in dominion was David; he had dominion over bears, lions, giants and nations. What was his secret?

Psalms 119:16(KJV)
I will delight myself in thy statutes: I will not forget thy word.

The bedrock of David's success was his affinity for God's word. He described his love for the Word as a deer panting for water. Whenever God spoke, it re-echoes in his ear making him hear more than once.

Psalms 62:11(KJV)

God hath spoken once; twice have I heard this; that power belongeth unto God.

In the fight for dominion, it was Jesus' grip of God's Word that brought victory. He kept saying 'it is written'. Jesus was not deficient in the Word. For instance, the deficiency of Vitamin A is the leading cause of preventable blindness in children; the deficiency of God's Word is the leading cause of spiritual blindness which causes one to fall into sin.

Psalms 119:11(KJV)

Thy word have I hid in mine heart, that I might not sin against thee.

When you hold on to God's word, nothing shakes you. Several years ago, in my twenties, I experienced a seeming asthmatic attack for three consecutive days, and it occurred at about the same time each night. It was as though I was unable to breathe, but I remembered God's word that I was not to die young. Hence, in the midst of the attack, I would laugh at the devil that I was not dying yet. Jesus was in a boat, in the midst of a storm, sleeping because he had a word that they were crossing over to the other side.

Mark 4:35-40(KJV)

And the same day, when the even was come, he saith unto them, Let us pass over unto the other side.

And when they had sent away the multitude, they took him even as he was in the ship. And there were also with him other little ships.

And there arose a great storm of wind, and the waves beat into the ship, so that it was now full.

And he was in the hinder part of the ship, asleep on a pillow: and they awake him, and say unto him, Master, carest thou not that we perish?

And he arose, and rebuked the wind, and said unto the sea, Peace, be still. And the wind ceased, and there was a great calm.

And he said unto them, Why are ye so fearful? how is it that ye have no faith?

The word was '*Let us pass over unto the other side*', it included everyone (us) in the boat. If the disciples had held on to that word, they would have been relaxed. They had no faith in the word, which is why Jesus asked, 'How is it that ye have no faith?'Jesus was so relaxed that the storm could not wake him. It took the disciples to wake him, so he had to calm the storm in order to calm them. A lot of people in auto crash die due to fear rather than the effects of the accident. A lot of people would live longer if they were calm and still. It is written, 'be still and know that I am the Lord'. In fact, for the Israelites to successfully cross the Red Sea, calmness was required of them; hence, Moses had to tell them, 'fear not, stand still'.

I travelled on an official assignment many years ago when my wife and children were involved in a terrible auto crash, a serious head-on collision. My wife had some of her rib bones broken; and had severe internal bleeding. God showed us mercy, and after some months, she was healed. I was giving the testimony in a fellowship; after which one of those in the medical team that attended to her informed me that my wife was almost gone but kept muttering the words 'I shall not die'. She held on to God's word till she got her life back. She had an anchor.

Hebrews 4:2(KJV)
For unto us was the gospel preached, as well as unto them: but the word preached did not profit them, not being mixed with faith in them that heard it.

Many folks hear the same word in meetings, but not everyone has the same effect on them because of how they receive the word. A good example is Jesus' parable of the sower. In the parable, the Scripture uses the clause, 'some seed' instead of 'some seeds', to signify that it was the same seed that the different grounds received. And that seed is the word, as explained in Mark 4:14.

Mark 4:3-8(AMP)

Give attention to this! Behold, a sower went out to sow.

And as he was sowing, some seed fell along the path, and the birds came and ate it up.

Other seed [of the same kind] fell on ground full of rocks, where it had not much soil; and at once it sprang up, because it had no depth of soil;

And when the sun came up, it was scorched, and because it had not taken root, it withered away.

Other seed [of the same kind] fell among thorn plants, and the thistles grew and pressed together and utterly choked and suffocated it, and it yielded no grain.

And other seed [of the same kind] fell into good (well-adapted) soil and brought forth grain, growing up and increasing, and yielded up to thirty times as much, and sixty times as much, and even a hundred times as much as had been sown.

Let me give another instance; I do minister to teenagers in Sunday school, and at the end of the year, a Bible based test is usually administered to them. In our teen's ministry, we call it 'Android Test'. The highest score above 80% attracts an android phone as the star prize. For some years no one had qualified to win the phone, but last year someone won it. The winner, in December 2018, wrote in our ministry chat group;

"I want to say a big thank you to uncle Abinye ... He said something that moved me... He said that he cannot write an examination and fail. I saw it as a challenge and here I am a winner with the Holy Spirit as my best friend..."

Several teenagers were in church when the statement was made, but just one teenager grasped it and challenged himself unto success. Abraham believed God, and it was counted as righteousness. Even when it did not look like it, but as God said it, Abraham held on till Isaac was born. Hold God's Word as an anchor, it is steadfast and sure. Ponder on a portion of this hymn;

Will your anchor hold in the storms of life,
When the clouds unfold their wings of strife?
When the strong tides lift, and the cables strain,
Will your anchor drift or firm remain?

We have an anchor that keeps the soul
Stedfast and sure while the billows roll,
Fastened to the Rock which cannot move,
Grounded firm and deep in the Savior's love.

3. Prayer

A quote credited to Ezra Taft Benson says, "He who kneels before God, can stand before any man." Kneeling is a posture that has represented prayer over the years, though it seems to be changing. The quote points to the fact that if you are a man of prayer, you then walk in dominion and fear no man. An example of a man of prayer was the Prophet Elijah; in him you could see dominion personified. He demonstrated the power to tell the rain when and for how long not to come down.

James 5:17-18(KJV)

Elias was a man subject to like passions as we are, and he prayed earnestly that it might not rain: and it rained not on the earth by the space of three years and six months.

And he prayed again, and the heaven gave rain, and the earth brought forth her fruit.

There are several books on prayer, written by wonderful men of God. This is not one of those books to teach you how to pray, yet there are some mysteries that God will reveal to you concerning prayer in the next few lines.

Prayer was so vital in the life of Jesus that he had to pray through the night sometimes. His disciples witnessed the effect of prayers such that they requested Jesus to teach them to pray. The effective prayer of a righteous man avails much. You can dominate your environment with prayer. You can change times and schedules. A friend of mine was working on his thesis or project and was experiencing unnecessary delays from his supervisor. A date had been proposed for the school's convocation and it would negatively affect him if he was not through with his project. He had put in his best effort, but the lecturer supervising him was just hard. He prayed and made a declaration that the convocation would not be held until he was ready for it. And true to his words, the date for the convocation kept being moved until he was ready. Were schedules changed in Scripture? Yes! Through prayer, Joshua was able to change times and seasons.

Joshua 10:12(CEV)

The LORD was helping the Israelites defeat the Amorites that day. So about noon, <u>Joshua prayed to the LORD</u> loud enough for the Israelites to hear: "Our LORD, make the sun stop in the sky over Gibeon, and the moon stand still over Aijalon Valley." <u>So the sun and the moon stopped and stood still</u> until Israel defeated its enemies. This poem can be found in The Book of Jashar. The sun stood still and didn't go down for about a whole day.

The way the contemporary English version puts it challenges me. Joshua prayed loud enough for the people to hear him. Some people would say it in their mind so that if the sun does not stand still, they would not be called fake prayer warriors. You can now imagine the reason so many believers cannot lay hands on sick people and command healing. Suppose nothing happens, makes them panic. Some years back, I had this problem until the Lord delivered me from that fear. Since then, I have experienced and seen people healed when my hands were laid on them. If you lay hands and nothing happens, simply go to the next person. Do not feel downcast and do not try to fake anything.

I was ministering God's Word on healing one Sunday morning in the Teenage Church, and I called those who were sick or had pains to come out. I started laying hands on them one after another. They were being healed as I asked them to check themselves after ministering healing. I then laid my hand on one young boy who said he had pains. 'Check yourself', I said; he said the pain was still there. I prayed again and laid hands on him again. The pain was still there, so I told him to go back while I prayed for others. If nothing happened, I would not just stand there, I jump and pass. After being through with the others, I asked him to come forward. He said he was already healed. In his words while testifying, he said, 'when I went back, I said to myself that if Uncle Abinye can be healing people, then I can too, and I prayed for myself and the healing happened'. Hallelujah! Some of the cases that make you run about looking for a prophet, you can handle them yourself as a believer.

Joshua changed the schedule of the Sun and Moon because he was a man of prayer. When the disciples asked Jesus to teach them how to pray, He gave them great principles for dominating and changing schedules to fit them through a parable.

Luke 11:1(KJV)

And it came to pass, that, as he was praying in a certain place, when he ceased, one of his disciples said unto him, Lord, teach us to pray, as John also taught his disciples.

Luke 11:5-8(KJV)

And he said unto them, Which of you shall have a friend, and shall go unto him at midnight, and say unto him, Friend, lend me three loaves;

For a friend of mine in his journey is come to me, and I have nothing to set before him?

And he from within shall answer and say, Trouble me not: the door is now shut, and my children are with me in bed; I cannot rise and give thee.

I say unto you, Though he will not rise and give him, because he is his friend, yet because of his importunity he will rise and give him as many as he needeth.

In the parable, the man went to his friend at midnight to make a request. Someone who is not a friend could sometimes make a request at a favourable hour, but not at midnight. He first had the audacity to go at that odd hour because he was a friend. It would have amounted to an abomination if he, coming at this unusual hour, was not a friend of the owner of the house. Consider a simple extrapolation; who is a friend of God? A friend of God is one who loves His Word and obeys Him.

John 15:14(KJV)
Ye are my friends, if ye do whatsoever I command you.

John 15:7 (KJV)

If ye abide in me, and my words abide in you, ye shall ask what ye will, and it shall be done unto you.

It implies that if you do not keep and obey God's word, you are none of His. Therefore at 'midnight', you have no reason to be at His doorstep.

Proverbs 28:9(KJV)

He that turneth away his ear from hearing the law, even his prayer shall be abomination.

In the midst of Jesus' busy schedule, a centurion needed Jesus to come and heal his servant. It was like a 'midnight' situation due to the busy schedule of Jesus. Yet those who came to meet Jesus on behalf of the man understood the principle of being a friend of God, and they said to Jesus in Luke 7:4 that "he was worthy for whom he should do this: For he loves our nation, and he hath built us a synagogue". Then Jesus went with them.

Getting back to the parable, the man arrived at his friend's house at midnight and received a predictable response. 'The door is now shut, and my children are with me in bed; I cannot rise and give thee', was the reply. The friend did not say he cannot give him the bread he requested. What he said, in essence, was that it would not be possible this night, come back in the morning. Here is the area where the principle Jesus wanted the disciples to learn comes in. The man kept knocking and was persistent. The owner of the house kept saying he should wait till the morning. Yet the 8th verse says that even if he will not get up and give him the bread because he is his friend, yet he will get up and give him everything he needs because he is not ashamed to keep on asking. A prayer of faith has what it takes to change schedules. Consider the miracle at the marriage in Cana, it was completely off schedule. The schedule to perform the miracle had not reached, but someone's persistence changed the timing.

John 2:1-5 (KJV)

And the third day there was a marriage in Cana of Galilee; and the mother of Jesus was there:

And both Jesus was called, and his disciples, to the marriage.

And when they wanted wine, the mother of Jesus saith unto him, They have no wine.

Jesus saith unto her, Woman, what have I to do with thee? mine hour is not yet come.

His mother saith unto the servants, Whatsoever he saith unto you, do it.

It looks like Jesus had a schedule from heaven for everything; hence, he told Mary that it was not yet his time. The mother seemingly ignored that statement and told the disciples to follow Jesus because by faith he must perform. As for me, I want my miracle now. While reading this book, you might have a situation either with your health or finances for which you trust that someday it would be better; become more deliberate in your request. What God can do tomorrow, He can also do it today. I went through a medical test that showed a challenge with my liver and was advised to watch my diet. I was hoping that in three months while following the medical advice, there would be great improvement from God. At that point, what I heard in my spirit was that if God can do it in three months, then He can heal you in one month. I held unto that, so that exactly one month later, I went back to the same clinic and went through the same two tests. This time, the tests showed that the condition was back to normal. I wish to address someone's condition; every abnormal condition in your body returns to normal in Jesus name.

CHAPTER 5

WALKING IN FINANCIAL DOMINION

When God said that man was to have dominion over the earth, it included all the subsystems or spheres in the earth. For the earth is the Lord's and its fullness thereof. The earth has different spheres such as the lithosphere (land), hydrosphere (water), biosphere (living things), and atmosphere (air); so there are also different areas where we can walk in dominion. Hence, we can walk in financial dominion, intellectual dominion, marital dominion and the list continues.

You must hate laziness to walk in financial dominion. You may have a catalogue of excuses, yet never be comfortable eating what you did not work for. It is written that a person who does not work should not eat. Okay! You are working and earning a salary; so you feel you have escaped laziness. Do you know that there are people who earn a living but are unable to provide for their families? There are others who have worked for years and, at the point of retiring, have nothing to show for the years. I really want to spur you to work, or rather, work harder.

1 Timothy 5:8 (KJV)

But if any provide not for his own, and specially for those of his own house, he hath denied the faith, and is worse than an infidel.

A man is required to provide for his family. You cannot have a blessed rest without providing for your home. God gave us a perfect example; during creation, He made everything man would need, then created man on the sixth day. Being that He had provided all that man needed, He rested on the seventh day. Parents would understand that when they are able to provide for their children; rest is sweet.

Genesis 1:28(KJV)

And God blessed them; and God said to them, Be fruitful and multiply, and fill the earth, and subdue it; and have dominion over the fish of the sea, and over the fowl of the heavens, and over every animal that moveth on the earth.

The key phrases in Genesis 1:28 preceding having dominion are 'be fruitful', 'multiply', and 'fill the earth and subdue it'. Being fruitful denotes the ability to produce resources; to multiply signifies expanding your business; to fill and subdue signifies having an overflow. I pointed out earlier that earning a salary does not necessarily mean you are not lazy. Look at the next scriptural verse.

Proverbs 12:27(KJV)

The slothful man roasteth not that which he took in hunting: but the substance of a diligent man is precious.

Another word for 'slothful' is 'lazy'. The lazy man in Proverbs 12:27 went out for hunting and brought in his substance just as a man goes to work and receives a salary. Yet the man was considered lazy because he did not process his substance wisely. Yes, you work and produce resources by earning a salary, yet you can be considered lazy if you do not go to the next level by using your income wisely. In this chapter, we will look at factors to consider when walking in financial dominion.

When man was created, everything was working well for his good; it was as though he was wired for auto-prosperity (it was not manual at all) for he was not to sweat before good things came into his path. He was constrained by his disobedience. The devil deceived the man. According to John 10:10; the devil (the thief) came to steal, kill, and destroy. The devil goes about like a roaring lion, seeking whom to devour and destroy. The devil hates to see you prosper; resist him and he shall flee away from you.

Psalms 105:15(KJV)

Saying, Touch not mine anointed, and do my prophets no harm.

The devil is in disobedience whenever he touches God's anointed; he walks in disobedience when he makes your business fail and makes you get down financially. What are you going to do, beloved?

2 Corinthians 10:6 (KJV)

And having in a readiness to revenge all disobedience, when your obedience is fulfilled.

You have the right to resist and revenge this satanic disobedience, but that can be done when your obedience to God's will is complete.

Isaiah 1:19(KJV)
If ye be willing and obedient, ye shall eat the good of the land:

Adam was freely eating the good of the land (Eden) until he disobeyed. If you want to partake of the good of the land, then you need to be obedient to God. Disobedience attracts limitations, while obedience removes them. There are several factors to consider concerning walking in financial dominion. I call them factors because they need to move together to give the desired result. In mathematics, if x and y are factors of a number, then the number may not be achieved by either x or y alone; they need to go hand in hand. Some of the factors are given below;

FACTOR 1: OBEY GOD

It is commonly said that if it is too good to be true, then it probably is. It is an idiom that expresses suspicion of people or situations that offer a large benefit for very little in return. As much as I appreciate the idiom, put it in mind that if it is God that says it, just obey. A good example was when there was an urgent need to make a payment and Jesus told Peter to visit a river to get some money.

Matthew 17:24-27 (KJV)

And when they were come to Capernaum, they that received tribute money came to Peter, and said, Doth not your master pay tribute?

He saith, Yes. And when he was come into the house, Jesus prevented him, saying, What thinkest thou, Simon? of whom do the kings of the earth take custom or tribute? of their own children, or of strangers?

Peter saith unto him, Of strangers. Jesus saith unto him, Then are the children free.

Notwithstanding, lest we should offend them, go thou to the sea, and cast an hook, and take up the fish that first cometh up; and when thou hast opened his mouth, thou shalt find a piece of money: that take, and give unto them for me and thee.

It is easy to look back in history and condemn Thomas for doubting the resurrection of Jesus; envisage it happening in our time. Also imagine that you were to pay a class fee and you met someone you respect to seek assistance; and the person said to you, 'go to the river, and cast a hook, and take up the first fish you catch, take money from its mouth, and make the payment'. What would be your reaction? If Peter had mentioned it to Matthew, perhaps he would have discouraged him and said that he would look for money somewhere else for Peter. It is time that we listen for the voice of God. If Judas saw Peter going towards the river, he would have laughed at him, not knowing what Jesus told him. Do not be quick to condemn someone; you may not know what God told the person. The disciples, at a time, verbally condemned a woman who broke an alabaster box of an extremely expensive ointment; meanwhile, she was commended by their Master.

Listen for God's voice. When God gives someone an instruction, it may be different from the instruction He will give to you. Captain Naaman of Syria expected that Elisha would mutter some words for his healing, but alas, he got a specific and customized instruction. That someone you trust joins an investment does not mean you must join. Listen for God's instruction.

God's instruction brings peace of mind. Also learn to hear well and differentiate between God's voice and the voice of greed. Luke 8:18 says 'take heed therefore how ye hear'.

Luke 5:3-7(GNT)

Jesus got into one of the boats---it belonged to Simon---and asked him to push off a little from the shore. Jesus sat in the boat and taught the crowd.

When he finished speaking, he said to Simon, "Push the boat out further to the deep water, and you and your partners let down your nets for a catch."

"Master," Simon answered, "we worked hard all night long and caught nothing. But if you say so, I will let down the nets."

They let them down and caught such a large number of fish that the nets were about to break.

So they motioned to their partners in the other boat to come and help them. They came and filled both boats so full of fish that the boats were about to sink.

Peter was a professional fisherman with a long time of experience. He had tried all night and had confirmed that fishes were not in that axis. Peter and his partners were understandably washing their nets. Then, Jesus came to them, saying that they should throw the nets into the water to catch fish. It might not have made sense to Peter, *nevertheless at His word* they throw the nets and got an overwhelming amount of fishes. It was a jaw-dropping, net-breaking, ship-sinking miracle. You may be an ICAN-certified financial analyst and the idea may not make sense, but IF GOD says go in, there is then no reason to fear. Listen for God's voice.

The word of God is good news (gospel); it comes with the power to make things good. God had a plan for light to be on the earth and he spoke the word – '*let there be light*'. It means that the Word accompanies God's plan. So, when God expresses that *His plan towards you is of good to give you an expected end,* He sends His word. For He sends forth His word and heals our diseases, I must tell you that the Scriptures are fully loaded for your good. What does a blind man need? It is sight. What does a lame man need? It is to walk. What does a leper need? It is to be cleansed of leprosy. What does a dead situation need? It is to be raised up. What do the poor need? Is it money or the word?

Matthew 11:5(KJV)

The blind receive their sight, and the lame walk, the lepers are cleansed, and the deaf hear, the dead are raised up, and the poor have the gospel preached to them.

The poor need the word to renew their minds. If you dole out money to a person with a negative mind-set, be sure that the money will go in the negative direction. There are people who you give millions in hard currency to start a business; after a year when you expect to receive their call to appreciate you, instead the call you receive is for you to assist them with more money for the business to survive. There are lots of such people around. Of course, 'the poor you will have with you always'.

If you desire to walk in financial dominion, open your mind to receive direction from God and prepare to obey Him. Consider the man, Isaac, who was in a land where things were considered hard. He premeditated prosperity in another place, but God told him to remain where he was, and he obeyed.

Genesis 26:1-3 (MSG)

There was a famine in the land, as bad as the famine during the time of Abraham. And Isaac went down to Abimelech, king of the Philistines, in Gerar.

GOD appeared to him and said, "Don't go down to Egypt; stay where I tell you.

Stay here in this land and I'll be with you and bless you. I'm giving you and your children all these lands, fulfilling the oath that I swore to your father Abraham.

Genesis 26:6(MSG)

So Isaac stayed put in Gerar.

Genesis 26:12-13

Isaac planted crops in that land and took in a huge harvest. GOD blessed him. The man got richer and richer by the day until he was very wealthy.

I have a feeling that when a man faces limitations and is frustrated, God would have spoken some instructions to him; but either the mind was not receptive or he heard but did not obey. As an illustration, for a vehicle to get bad on the road or for the tyre to pull out, it must have given the driver a sign; the sign could be a light or sound indication.

That you did not understand an instruction is not an excuse. Through a dream, God gave a sign to Pharoah of a coming challenge through Joseph. He did not understand it, but made an effort till he got Joseph. In fact, the same message came twice, just like David would say, "Once have you spoken, and twice I have heard'

Genesis 41:32(MSG)
The fact that Pharaoh dreamed the same dream twice emphasizes God's determination to do this and do it soon.

Joseph interpreted the dream and gave further advice to Pharoah. They walked in financial and economic dominion as a result of their obedience to the instruction.

Genesis 41:32-36(KJV)
And for that the dream was doubled unto Pharaoh twice; it is because the thing is established by God, and God will shortly bring it to pass.

Now therefore let Pharaoh look out a man discreet and wise, and set him over the land of Egypt.

Let Pharaoh do this, and let him appoint officers over the land, and take up the fifth part of the land of Egypt in the seven plenteous years.

And let them gather all the food of those good years that come, and lay up corn under the hand of Pharaoh, and let them keep food in the cities.

And that food shall be for store to the land against the seven years of famine, which shall be in the land of Egypt; that the land perish not through the famine.

Pharoah obeyed, and the result is already known. Indeed, there is wisdom in saving. The Bible makes it clear that wisdom is profitable to direct. There is a trait we all need; it is the ability to save money. In my book, *Creating Your Season of Abundance,* I mentioned having an emergency fund and other kinds of savings. It takes wisdom to do that. In his book, *The Money Challenge,* Art Rainer gives practical reasons to give generously, save wisely, and live appropriately. The major reason that ants are considered wise in the Bible is their ability to save.

Proverbs 21:20 (TLB)

The wise man saves for the future, but the foolish man spends whatever he gets.

Proverbs 30:24-25 (BBE)

There are four things which are little on the earth, but they are very wise:

The ants are a people not strong, but they put by a store of food in the summer;

FACTOR 2: KNOWLEDGE

The factor, knowledge can be viewed from various angles. One of the angles is that of knowing your heritage in Christ.

The Bible points out in Proverbs 13:22 that a good man leaves an inheritance to his children's children; which could mean that that good man leaves more than enough for his children, so it spills over to another generation. In other words, the inheritance being more than enough for his children had to extend to his children's children. Can you imagine how far God will go for His children?

Matthew 7:11(KJV)

If ye then, being evil, know how to give good gifts unto your children, how much more shall your Father which is in heaven give good things to them that ask him?

A man can leave a great sum of money for a child, and the child, unaware of the heritage, would be eating crumbs. When you are not aware of the goodly heritage which God has apportioned to you, you will settle for mediocrity. If God has predestined you to own a factory but you settle for a roadside kiosk out of fear, you deserve to be queried.

Psalms 16:5-6(KJV)

The LORD is the portion of mine inheritance and of my cup: thou maintainest my lot.

The lines are fallen unto me in pleasant places; yea, I have a goodly heritage.

Being ignorant of your heritage can be worse than having a broken ankle. When you do not know how far you can reach, you throw away opportunities. For instance, you have an opportunity to go for certification training, and you wonder why you should pay for such training when you do not believe you could rise to the position of director. Soon, your juniors become your boss, and then all you can do is pray in church that all those taking your seat should die by fire and thunder. Wake up. The Scriptures say, "Arise – Shine". When a goat is tied to a tree, it tries to move beyond the length of the rope and is pulled back. Hence, it is restricted by the rope around a limited circumference. When it has gotten used to the limits, it becomes mental slavery; such that even when the rope is no longer there, it does not attempt to go beyond the initial limit. Some people have gotten used to the fact that their parents never experienced financial dominion, so when they see opportunities they believe it is not for their lineage.

Ephesians 1:11-12(KJV)
In whom also we have obtained an inheritance, being predestinated according to the purpose of him who worketh all things after the counsel of his own will:

That we should be to the praise of his glory, who first trusted in Christ.

Great words with great implications are imbedded in the Scriptures. It is to one's detriment to ignore the small print in a legal document, especially one issued by a bank. Check out the following documentation in the Bible.

2 Corinthians 8:9(KJV)

For ye know the grace of our Lord Jesus Christ, that, though he was rich, yet for your sakes he became poor, that ye through his poverty might be rich.

Some folks apparently boast of their poverty, saying that Jesus was also poor. Was Jesus poor? Yes, in that He became poor for a purpose—so that we would be rich. I am taking the Scripture as it is; it's not my own interpretation. He gave out the inheritance. The gift was sacrificial. Consider a father: The father spent all he had to send his son to school to be worthwhile. The father could not build a house or own a car like others, just to be able to train his son. After so many years, the boy came out worthless and uneducated. How would the father feel? How would the Lord feel if his becoming poor did not translate to his desired outcome? A vivid knowledge of your heritage from God should spur you to do the right thing; trusting God, working effectively, and prospering. Can I add that a true believer should not be lazy?

Another angle of knowledge is having the requisite know-how for any business you have put your hands to do. It is written in the Scriptures that people are destroyed for lack of knowledge; similarly, businesses are destroyed for lack of knowledge. It is proper to have adequate knowledge in the field of business in which you are engaged. If a man travels a distance to meet a tailor to sew an agbada (a native attire), and the tailor says he does not know how to sew that; another day, the same man comes to inquire if he can sew a French suit, and the tailor has no knowledge of that, the man may never spend his transport coming to that tailor again. Even if you do not specialize in an area in your field, you should have enough knowledge to give advice to help the customer.

Some people use the internet to watch comedies alone; hence, it becomes a liability instead of an asset. Imagine meeting a restaurant chef with a million dollar contract to prepare a pepper soup dish for some days for some guests, and the chef says that he has no knowledge of cooking pepper soup. In these days when you have tutorials on several dishes on YouTube and other websites; such a chef would spend time in churches asking that hands be laid on him/her for breakthrough.

When you see someone always looking back during an examination; it is a sign that the individual lacks knowledge and is looking for an opportunity to copy. Let me blend it with the Scripture that says 'No man, having put his hand to the plough, and looking back, is fit ...'; if you put your hands in a business and lack adequate knowledge, you are not fit. God blesses the work of your hands for which you show diligence and competence.

Proverbs 18:15(MSG)
Wise men and women are always learning, always listening for fresh insights.

Proverbs 15:14(GNT)
Intelligent people want to learn, but stupid people are satisfied with ignorance.

These Scriptures go straight to the point. Intelligent people never claim to know it all; they are always seeking an opportunity to learn more. It is said that the day you stop learning is the day you start dying. Fresh insights are like radio waves moving everywhere, and wise men and women set up their antennas to connect. You must note that it is not everyone on the internet that is browsing for something useful. It is not everyone with a newspaper that is reading; if you look closely, the paper may be upside down. Be focused when seeking information. Because the devil is known as the prince of the air, he is skilled at manipulating the airwaves and has embedded numerous distractions in the airwaves/internet.

The next Scripture is here, put forth, in two translations to bring forth a better insight. Some people are parsimonious when it comes to spending money to improve themselves.

Proverbs 23:23(ERV)
Truth, wisdom, learning, and understanding are worth paying money for. They are worth far too much to ever sell.

Proverbs 23:23(CEV)
Invest in truth and wisdom, discipline and good sense, and don't part with them.

When it comes to improving yourself, do not procrastinate. There are several materials, such as books or videos, on any field; both hard and soft copies. Buy materials and do not just depend on free materials. Do not get me wrong; there are some wonderful free training materials, but do not procrastinate your training just because you have to pay for it. When I needed to learn to play a particular musical instrument, I sourced and paid for a training course on the *Udemy.com* website. After that, I bought several training materials on different areas from that website though I am not paid to advertise them, when one has information, it is good to share.

Invest in truth and wisdom, discipline and good sense. Buy and read books. My personal library is currently overflowing with books. My laptop is also packed with videos and documents in areas I need improvement.

FACTOR 3: WORK

The third factor is to WORK; in other words, more action and less talking. No matter how potent faith is, it is clearly written in the Scriptures that faith without works is dead. There are people who want to claim everything by faith without working; they see someone wearing a beautiful pair of shoes and say something like 'I claim your shoes by faith'. An epitome of faith, Paul, said that he who does not work should not eat, no matter the faith status.

There are several tricksters parading in churches today because they want to eat without working. It is so unfortunate that some of them put on collars. It is not news that people have built houses through begging, but to work is more honourable. May God bless the works of your hands. And it is this blessing of God that gives you financial dominion without sorrow.

Proverbs 10:22(KJV)
The blessing of the LORD, it maketh rich, and he addeth no sorrow with it.

Talk less and work better. Some people spend more time talking than doing the necessary work. One of the commands in James 1:19 is for us to be slow to speak. Being slow to speak gives you more time to work. There are people who, instead of making their business grow, are always complaining that others are using charm to prosper. This is common with people in the same line of business. What does the Bible say?

1 John 4:4(KJV)

Ye are of God, little children, and have overcome them: because greater is he that is in you, than he that is in the world.

What you have in you, as a person of dominion, is greater than any charm. So instead of murmuring, show what is in you. Moses did not complain about the number of people in Pharoah's palace using charms. Those using charm threw their rods on the floor; and the rods became snakes. Moses' rod was already on the floor and had swallowed all the other snakes, and still 'no shaking'. Less talk, more action.

I made up my mind from my secondary school days and beyond to stay away from all forms of examination malpractice. There were people who I knew were very brilliant yet were involved in malpractice or 'expo' as we called it then. I didn't have to talk about them, but I did make an effort to study hard. There are people who, instead of studying, go round complaining and telling the teachers or lecturers that so-and-so copied in the exam, so-and-so cheated... Does that sound familiar? I remember clearly praying and saying to God, 'I am not bothered about those cheating, but Lord, where ever their cheating will take them in terms of marks, make my marks higher than theirs'. And I went ahead, studying hard; God, being faithful, honoured me. I was always at the top.

Failure is actually a bad thing; it has a way of affecting one's mentality. When a student fails continually, he/she starts to feel that anyone who succeeds must have compromised the faith. Succeeding through wrong means is even worse; it makes one feel that others' success must have been through the same means. Someone says that to a man with yellow fever, everything appears yellow. On the other hand, though, when you have a good heart, you feel everyone else has a good heart too. I was interviewing and counselling someone; from the discussion, I observed the person was not sound in maths; I was shocked because the WAEC result showed an 'A' in maths. The reason I was shocked was that I was the best in maths in my final year in secondary school and got an 'A' in maths; so whenever I see someone having such a grade in maths, I get excited. It was only after some questioning that the confession came in that someone else had written that particular paper for the counselee. The result was different, and the fruit was different. It is said that 'by their fruits you shall know them'. Less talk, more action.

I saw this quote in a book; It is rain that grows flowers, not thunder. So learn to be quiet, and affect your world for good with your actions.

1 Thessalonians 4:11(KJV)
And that ye study to be quiet, and to do your own business, and to work with your own hands, as we commanded you

In this passage, Paul gave three straight commands, which is a bedrock for walking in financial dominion.

- *study to be quiet*
- *do your own business*
- *work with your own hands*

These commands are summarized in the point made earlier; less talking, more actions. Let us consider Paul's commands in some details.

Quietness is a principle: it is a course that needs studying. Do not be shy about going through the course, Quietness 101. So many people have misfired by talking too much. It is said that in the multitude of words, sin is not lacking. It is not everyone to whom you tell your dream or vision, especially in its early stages. Some people are well calibrated as vision extinguishers. Have you not heard of cases where a man tells his friend of a song he would like to release, and the friend goes around releasing the song first as a "single"? There are people who you give your manuscript to, and before you know it, they have published the work.

Someone may be resentful, asking if he should not talk again. As a child then, I heard people say if you do not talk, one could have a stinky mouth. Learning to be quiet is strategic. There is a difference between the words: quiet and silence. Silence means no sound, but quiet is less talk and talking with wisdom when necessary. Quietness needs to be studied, hence the command: study to be quiet.

Mind or do your own business: Most of the different translation of 1 Thessalonians 4:11 did not skip the word "own". It demands that you focus on your own job. Let us consider the scenario; you sat for an examination and the instruction was to answer three out of five questions. Answering the whole five questions does not give you more marks. The extra two were not your "own" questions. When you mind your own job, you tend to do it better.

There are evangelists who, before God, should have gone from village to village evangelizing, but instead chose to build and pastor a church; some of those churches no longer exist. Imagine a traffic warden leaving his control of traffic to begin checking vehicle particulars and molesting motorists. If you are paid to be a teacher in school, improve yourself in this 'your own job' than start bringing items to class to sell to your students. If you are in the children's ministry, concentrate and do not go about looking for other appointments in the church. I was once the organist in the assembly where I worshipped and also doubled as a children's ministry teacher, but I had to leave being the organist to focus on the children's ministry, where I felt God's call. And as I focused, I felt more grace and unction upon me. Am I speaking against diversifying? NO! Far from it. What Paul is saying is that if a duty is assigned to you or you are being paid to do a job; focus on it first and effectively before doing the extras. If you do the extras, you will most likely be noticed, but if you do not perform well on the job, you will not be rewarded. Consider taking your car to a mechanic to fix an issue with your brakes; you gave him two hours to do the repair because you needed to go on a journey with the vehicle; the mechanic notices that your car is very dirty, so he washes the car sparkling clean; he also changes the dull-looking wiper to a more fashionable one. Two hours later, you return to see your car sparkling, but the brake has not been repaired. How will you react? Be the judge. I believe you understand the command better now; do your own business.

Work with your own hands: We are all endowed with skills and talents, but some people do not bother developing and utilizing their skills. There are several employment needs that could be met if we all harness our God-given talents. For every employment opportunity you desire to have, someone created that job. You have what it takes to create jobs and employ others. One sure factor that hinders people from working with their own hands is the fear of failure. Do not just sit back, make an attempt. A quote credited to Vincent van Gogh says, 'What would life be if we had no courage to attempt anything?' Imagine what stress the universe would have been through and for how long if Thomas Edison had not contributed to society his own quota of persistence.

Henry Ford made a profound statement that 'one who fears failure limits his activities. Failure is only the opportunity to more intelligently begin again'. Also, George Edward Woodberry inputs, 'Defeat is not the worst of failures. Not to have tried is the true failure'. A lady came to my home, introduced herself as a launderer. She goes around getting dirty clothes, washing and ironing them for a fee. That was good, though I did not give her any clothes because, as I told her; I do wash and iron myself. Frankly speaking, there are things that we have the time and ability to do ourselves that we pay for. Learn to work with your own hands.

Students in school could learn to do petty trades to cover some bills. Many years ago, I was making and selling a local nutritious drink called 'Zobo'. I became a major supplier of the drink in my locality as a young person. At another time, I was a dealer in phone network recharge cards. I was not beggarly. Less talking and more action is what the average young person needs. There will be a lot of discouraging moments, but keep on learning.

James 1:19(KJV)
Wherefore, my beloved brethren, let every man be swift to hear, slow to speak, slow to wrath:

Swift to hear (show ability to learn fast)

Slow to speak (learn quietness)

Slow to wrath (slow to being discouraged and avoid being easily angered)

FACTOR 4: GIVE

Dominion has to do with being on top. Is there an authoritative statement that indicates that givers stay on top? Well, the Bible is the authority on which this factor is based.

Proverbs 22:7(NLT)
Just as the rich rule the poor, so the borrower is servant to the lender.

The borrower is the one who receives, while the lender gives. The lender in the above verse has a form of dominion over the borrower. Some folks cannot comprehend lending to be a form of 'giving'; but it is. There are people who desperately need to start a business, and the loan you provide is the miracle they require. You may not have noticed the next Scripture before;

Psalms 37:26(NLT)
The godly always give generous loans to others, and their children are a blessing.

Deuteronomy 15:6(NKJV)

For the Lord your God will bless you just as He promised you; you shall lend to many nations, but you shall not borrow; you shall reign over many nations, but they shall not reign over you.

Also perceive what the Deuteronomy passage says; you shall lend to nations ... you shall reign over nations. To reign means dominion. There is a shift in your dominion status when you give or lend to others. Many people in the world understand the principle and use it to their advantage. Some elders in the village have no say over certain issues because they are recipient of gifts from people they should have corrected and disciplined. Some pastors cannot preach some messages because they are now financial slaves to certain members. It may shock you to be aware that those in charge of some churches are not the pastors but some occultic rich men who have invested their cash in the church. There was a lament in the Bible that "the sons of the world are for their own generation wiser than the children of light" (Luke 16:8).

As an advice, you must be careful where and from whom you borrow money. Some wicked men, who understand the principle of lenders having dominion, consciously and intentionally advertise that people borrow from them. And when you fall for it, you may never be able to fully pay it back; you just remain a slave to them. There are countless people around us who are slaves to banks.

Acts 20:35(BBE)

In all things I was an example to you of how, in your lives, you are to give help to the feeble, and keep in memory the words of the Lord Jesus, how he himself said, There is a greater blessing in giving than in getting.

The cost of receiving and borrowing can be very high. Think of Gehazi, the servant of Elisha, who received a gift from the hands of Naaman and the cost he had to pay. Reflect on Esau, who received what cost him his birthright. People have now become believers just for what they will get. It's shocking that some people now preach in transport vehicles with the motive of cajoling people to put money in their polythene bags.

I thank God for my wife, who has the ever fresh grace to preach in vehicles without having to call for money.

I once read a statement by Harold Herring that "God does not prosper us for the purpose of raising our *standard of living*. He prospers us so that we can raise our *standard of giving*." Hence, when you are a giver, God blesses you.

2 Corinthians 9:11(TLB)
"Yes, God will give you much so that you can give away much, ..."

My elder sister, Dr Chinyere Almona, in one of her books, quoted Zig Ziglar as having said, " You can have everything in life you want, if you will just help enough other people get what they want." This statement really resonated with me. The Bible says that give and it shall be given to you, good measure ... would men give into your bosom. It is usually said that givers never lack. Be a giver and be a help to someone. As shown in Matthew 25, on the last day, Jesus would be more interested in the help you gave to people around you.

Matthew 25:34-36(TLB)

"Then I, the King, shall say to those at my right, 'Come, blessed of my Father, into the Kingdom prepared for you from the founding of the world.

For I was hungry and you fed me; I was thirsty and you gave me water; I was a stranger and you invited me into your homes;

naked and you clothed me; sick and in prison, and you visited me.'

It is frightening to note that some believers would be shut out of the Kingdom. Those who were invited to enter the Kingdom were not those who answered an altar call or attended fellowship regularly. They were asked to enter for... or because of... verse 35.

Readers don't get furious at me here, I was only quoting what Jesus said. Sometimes we can hold on to a word out of context. What I believe Jesus is emphasizing is that it is easier for a carmel to go through the eye of a needle than for a rich man (who is not a giver or helper) to enter the Kingdom of God. In all this, remember that it is God that is the judge and not man.

I came across a review of a German study titled, "Is Volunteering Rewarding in Itself?" by *Stephan Meier* and *Alois Stutzer*. The study shows that people who are generous and invest their time and resources for others have greater satisfaction in life than people who do not. And as Mary McCoy puts it in one of her online posts, "communities of people with high levels of giving tend to demonstrate greater satisfaction within the community than groups of people who do not give generously."

FACTOR 5: SAVINGS

You tend to beg when you do not have. When you do not have, you become subject to decisions of those who do.

Matthew 25:8(TLB)

...then the five who hadn't any oil begged the others to share with them, for their lamps were going out.

I pray that the eyes of your understanding will be enlightened. After this segment, may you hate being silly... sorry, did I say silly?

Matthew 25:7-8(MSG)

"The ten virgins got up and got their lamps ready. The silly virgins said to the smart ones, 'Our lamps are going out; lend us some of your oil.'

Saving money can save you from embarrassment. It can serve as a safety net in the case of an emergency. I have heard of people who, due to a severe need, had to do away with their landed properties at a ridiculously cheap price. Let me echo the words of Jesus, that he who does not have (savings), even what he has, will be taken away from him. I believe you can now see that Scripture in a new light.

Savings are meant to face and cushion future challenges. Recall Joseph and Pharaoh's encounter in the Bible. There was then a future famine challenge, and by divine wisdom, Joseph informed Pharaoh that by saving 20% of their income, the seven years of famine could be adequately cushioned. The challenge ahead determines what percentage of savings is necessary. If it is the challenge of buying a car, then you factor what it would take. But unfortunately, most future challenges are unplanned for; they come as emergencies. Sometimes it is a terrible health issue, the loss of a job, or the collapse of a business. It is important that you save so that if you lose a job or a business collapses, you have an amount to sustain you till you get another job.

If your income is meagre, it would sound funny to talk about savings, especially when you can hardly make ends meet. But the cost of not saving can be deadly. Saving money requires a lot of discipline. However, with firm determination, it is not a difficult habit to adopt. Saving money is worth the effort. It gives you peace of mind when you can knock off emergencies without having to beg and borrow. There are times when opportunities come as emergencies. Think of it; there could be an auction of a land you had desired for a little fee or a great investment opportunity and because you were unable to raise the fund within specified period, someone else gained from it. It is similar to the case of the silly vs smart virgins or the wise vs foolish virgins in Scripture.

"Do not save what is left after spending; instead spend what is left after saving." - Warren Buffett. An inability to save money is a sign that money controls you. There was a man in my neighbourhood many years back; whenever his salary is paid, he gets drunk, sometimes falling into the gutter. We use him to know when workers have been paid. Such a man is controlled by money. At once money comes; it pushes him to take an action. On the other hand, a man who controls money can tell his money to sit down first, and then direct the money where to go. That sounds like budgeting. Budgeting is telling your money what to do and when.

Are you smart or silly? A silly person spends all that comes to him with no recourse to saving. A smart person saves a part of his income in case of emergencies. Even ants are considered wise because they take savings seriously.

Proverbs 6:8-9 (GNT)

but they store up their food during the summer, getting ready for winter.

Tips for saving money

Save all unexpected money: Do not be quick to spend any bonus given to you especially when you had not expected it. Some people spend any money that drops into their bank account even without knowing who sent it. Someone was to celebrate his birthday and had made the necessary plans. Then a large sum dropped into his account, and he withdrew it and increased what he was to buy for the celebration. During the program, some people came with a policeman to arrest him. A banker had mistakenly mistyped an account number, and the money dropped, and before the banker could undo it, the money had been withdrawn. It became an issue; I had to intervene in the matter.

Purchase off-brand products and save the money: There are product brands that are expensive for which there are other brands or companies doing the same products which are cheaper. For instance, two laptops may have the same specifications but different prices due to different manufacturers.

Compare the costs of major items before purchase: I was to buy a gift for my wife during the Mothering Sunday celebrations. I was driving to a supermarket where I would usually purchase the item. While going, I passed another supermarket, and I decided to reverse and simply find out the cost there. It was about $30 (N11,000 at the time). I, then, continued my journey to the supermarket where I had proposed purchasing the item. Same product, same manufacturer and it was at $52 (N19,000 at the time). Where should I buy it? Your guess is as good as reality. When you carry out due diligence by comparing prices, it gives you an opportunity to save. Do not put yourself in a situation where you are always in a hurry to pay for items.

There are several ways of saving money, such as in thrifts and cooperatives. Also, there are other factors, which include investing, which are covered in my book titled, "CREATING YOUR SEASON OF ABUNDANCE".

CHAPTER 6

WALKING IN INTELLECTUAL DOMINION

An online dictionary defined intelligence as the ability to acquire and apply knowledge and skills. Man was created to be a master over all animals. We were made to be intellectually above all other creatures. That is why the statement about going to the ant to learn was specifically aimed at a specific group of people: the lazy.

Genesis 1:28-29(TLB)

And God blessed them and told them, "Multiply and fill the earth and subdue it; you are masters of the fish and birds and all the animals.

Many folks are satisfied with being average students or scholars. We are called to be different and not average. It is written that you should come out from among them (the average) and be different. An offshoot of God's blessing is for us to be masters; say no to mediocrity. We have a responsibility to be at the top of the class and never at the bottom. Some believers use their faith as an excuse to explain their low grades: O man, thou art inexcusable. Some have the wrong notion that faith and intelligence are mutually exclusive.

Deuteronomy 28:13-14(NLT)

If you listen to these commands of the Lord your God that I am giving you today, and if you carefully obey them, the Lord will make you the head and not the tail, and you will always be on top and never at the bottom.

If you can see and understand the blessings of God, you will hate failure. As a child of God, we should crave for success. When I read the story of the donkey that spoke intelligently to Balaam, I tell myself that it is an error for me to be intellectually down.

Numbers 22:28-30(MSG)

Then God gave speech to the donkey. She said to Balaam: "What have I ever done to you that you have beat me these three times?"

Balaam said, "Because you've been playing games with me! If I had a sword I would have killed you by now."

The donkey said to Balaam, "Am I not your trusty donkey on whom you've ridden for years right up until now? Have I ever done anything like this to you before? Have I?" He said, "No."

If God could give speech to a donkey, would he withhold success from you in your language classes? If the Almighty can care for sparrows, then He surely will take care of you through your academic undertakings. Do not be discouraged by the present situation if you are not at the level you desire. At a point in my secondary school days, I was academically down, especially in mathematics. I was at the bottom; but following some steps which I have also put in this book, with God being my helper, I became the top of my class in mathematics by my final year in secondary school. Meditate on this hymn.

Why should I feel discouraged,
Why should the shadows come,
Why should my heart be lonely,
And long for heaven and home,
When Jesus is my portion?
My constant friend is He:
His eye is on the sparrow, And I know He watches me;
His eye is on the sparrow, and I know He watches me.

I sing because I'm happy,
I sing because I'm free,
For His eye is on the sparrow,
And I know He watches me.

Let not your heart be troubled,
His tender word I hear,
And resting on His goodness,
I lose my doubts and fears;
Though by the path He leadeth,
But one step I may see;
His eye is on the sparrow, And I know He watches me;
His eye is on the sparrow, And I know He watches me.

Whenever I am tempted,
whenever clouds arise,
When songs give place to sighing,
when hope within me dies,
I draw the closer to Him,
from care He sets me free;
His eye is on the sparrow, And I know He watches me;
His eye is on the sparrow, And I know He watches me.

Keys to Intellectual/Academic Dominion

1. AVOID LAZINESS

Proverbs 6:6 (KJV)

Go to the ant, thou sluggard; consider her ways, and be wise:

Mr. Sluggard needs to go to the ant to learn. Frankly speaking, we need to open up the meaning of some names. The name Sluggard looks sweet till you look at other versions of Scripture. Let us take that verse from another translation of the Bible.

Proverbs 6:6 (MSG)

You lazy fool, look at an ant. Watch it closely; let it teach you a thing or two.

When God created man, He gave him dominion to be over all creatures and to be a master (teacher) to all animals. But from Proverbs 6:6, a lazy man has lost the mastery level and is to summit to the tutelage of an ant. In fact, if you send a lazy man to school, you will experience the discomforting situation as when smoke enters the eyes.

Proverbs 10:26 (NIV)

As vinegar to the teeth and smoke to the eyes, so is a sluggard to those who send him.

Let us consider the characteristics of the ant highlighted in Proverbs 6, that is to be considered a revival message to the lazy student.

Proverbs 6:6-8 (MSG)

You lazy fool, look at an ant. Watch it closely; let it teach you a thing or two. Nobody has to tell it what to do. All summer it stores up food; at harvest it stockpiles provisions.

Nobody has to tell the ant what to do. It just knows that it should be storing food (knowledge) while waiting for the difficult time. Some students wait for the examination timetable to be published before they start aggressive study. That is a form of laziness. Diligent students would not wait for a timetable to tell them what to do. A diligent student would study ahead of the lecturer. When you study a topic before it is taught in class, you ask the most brilliant questions and you understand the teaching better. A lazy student will not take time to do his academic assessments till it is time for submission, then he will start running up and down.

Sometimes the wicked devil works overtime on lazy students. When it is examination period, the student falls sick. A student who has read enough before the exam period, even when sickness shows up at the last hour, still excels, and that disgraces the devil. The greatest way of deliverance is when you disgrace the devil. Just like Jesus made a public show of the devil. When the devil tries with sickness and you are still succeeding because you studied ahead, he leaves. Bringing that exam sickness becomes a waste of resources for the devil, being a stingy personality. But for a lazy student who only reads during the examination period, the devil may find fun in dishing out exam sickness. This is not to mean that anyone who experiences sickness during an exam is automatically tagged as lazy. No, but let us all do our part to be diligent.

A diligent person puts in extra time. My junior secondary mathematics grade was a major source of concern for me. I decided to put in extra time to study mathematics. It paid off; I performed so well on a math test in class that my mathematics teacher summoned me to the staff room and informed the physics teacher that I am a genius and a serious student. That alone made me go back to studying Physics very well to prove that the maths teacher said the truth, and it paid off, as I then became excellent in Physics class; the physics teacher told the Chemistry teacher that I was a very brilliant star. I had to show due diligence in Chemistry also, and it paid off. Diligence pays.

Proverbs 22:29 (KJV)
Seest thou a man diligent in his business? he shall stand before kings; he shall not stand before <u>mean</u> men.

The word 'mean' means 'average'. A diligent man is not an average man; he is an on-top man. The diligent student is not a mediocre; he is an exceptional student.

2. SPEAK POSITIVELY AND MEAN IT

Proverbs 18:21 (MSG)
Words kill, words give life; they're either poison or fruit —you choose.

There are people who are intellectually dead due to the words they conceived and spoke. The things we say may look like nothing, but you would be surprised at their manifestation.

James 3:5 (MSG)

A word out of your mouth may seem of no account, but it can accomplish nearly anything — or destroy it! It only takes a spark, remember, to set off a forest fire.

Esau despised his birth right by saying, 'What good is the birth right to me?'. In fact, Jacob, knowing the power of words, required that Esau should say it again more clearly, as in a vow.

Genesis 25:33 (GNT)

Jacob answered, "First make a vow that you will give me your rights." Esau made the vow and gave his rights to Jacob.

If you study the Scripture, you may understand that Esau felt the words carried no weight until his eyes were open to the realities. Similarly, when the Israelites left Egypt, they opened their mouths to say things like "it is better we died than starve in the wilderness," and God responded with "Amen" to their prayer (words).

Numbers 14:2 (NKJV)

And all the children of Israel complained against Moses and Aaron, and the whole congregation said to them, "If only we had died in the land of Egypt! Or if only we had died in this wilderness!

Numbers 14:28-30 (NKJV)

Say to them, 'As I live,' says the Lord, 'just as you have spoken in My hearing, so I will do to you: 29 The carcasses of you who have complained against Me shall fall in this wilderness, all of you who were numbered, according to your entire number, from twenty years old and above.

Beloved, if God says 'amen' to everything you have said this month, what will your life be like? On the other hand, the situation you find yourself in now could be as a result of statements made through your lips. Parents should not be calling their kids "empty heads". Even when things aren't going well, speak positively about your children and call those things that be not as though they were. The Bible says that you shall speak to a mountain to be moved and it will go. Words have tremendous power.

Mark 11:23(KJV)

For verily I say unto you, That whosoever shall say unto this mountain, Be thou removed, and be thou cast into the sea; and shall not doubt in his heart, but shall believe that those things which he saith shall come to pass; he shall have whatsoever he saith.

I labelled this key — speak positively and with conviction. It is possible to speak without meaning it. The Scripture Mark 11:23 declares "*say... and... not doubt in his heart*". This means—"mean what you say". Many times, when people say negative things about themselves, they mean it. Practically reflect on it: When a person says "this situation is just impossible", his mind is in agreement. "I will try, but I know I will fail," their minds agree.

On the other hand, people say positive things and their minds are saying something else. Someone could say, "It will take a miracle for me to pass this exam" – it sounds positive, but the mind could be saying – I know I will fail this exam. The heart/mind is a vital element to your speaking, for it is written that from the abundance of the heart, the mouth speaks. It is also written that as a man thinks in his heart, so is he. Therefore, configure your mind to be positive and speak forth with that positivity. Refrain from saying anything negative.

1 Peter 3:10 (KJV)

For he that will love life, and see good days, let him refrain his tongue from evil, and his lips that they speak no guile:

3. CONSCIOUSLY MAKE YOUR LIGHT SHINE

Proverbs 31:18 (NKJV)

She perceives that her merchandise is good, And her lamp does not go out by night.

The Bible portrayed an intelligent woman, popularly called the Virtuous Woman. She consciously made her light shine. We have virtuous scholars in academia also. They are not tired of shining and they go from strength to strength. There are intelligent lecturers who are not tired of research and the publication of their findings. You can't be lazy and shine your light at the same time. Hence, the Bible says—arise, shine. You need to arise, be up and doing to shine forth.

Matthew 5:16 (KJV)

Let your light so shine before men, that they may see your good works, and glorify your Father which is in heaven.

The phrase "so shine" signifies excellence. Let your results be significantly excellent. Remember the case of Daniel and his friends; they were ten times better than their other colleagues in Babylon. No wonder it was said of Daniel that an excellent spirit was in him. He glorified God through his success.

So deliberately make your light shine. Men should be able to see your good works, which means your results should speak for you. You may claim to be a brilliant scholar with a 'but' in your results – NO. If your results are bad, no one would want to glorify God on your behalf. Do not give me that lyrics of being very busy for God and how it affected your academic results. What you are saying is that your work for God does not amount to glorifying God.

Proverbs 4:18(KJV)

But the path of the just is as the shining light, that shineth more and more unto the perfect day.

Do not be a mediocre; rather, keep shining more and more. And let men see your good results and glorify your Father who is in heaven.

4. PLACE YOUR GOALS BEFORE YOU

Hebrews 12:2(MSG)

Keep your eyes on Jesus, who both began and finished this race we're in. Study how he did it. Because he never lost sight of where he was headed — that exhilarating finish in and with God — he could put up with anything along the way: cross, shame, whatever. And now he's there, in the place of honor, right alongside God.

Can we study how Jesus achieved his goal? He never lost sight of his goal, for he always placed his goal before him. When asked what grade they would graduate with, some students at the entry level of tertiary institutions appear surprised. They feel it is too early to ask or determine. In the ideal sense, one should have a goal before entering school. The final grade starts with the first test and examination.

There are footballers who, after scoring a goal, go down with a serious injury. That injury came earlier, but seeing the goal in front of them, they had to keep moving and acquire that feat before permitting the injury to have its effect on them. The Scripture said Jesus could put up with anything, be it the cross or shame, in order to achieve his goal. Some students want to feel like they are among the big shots, hence they go to parties at the expense of their careers; their goal is not before them.

Joseph, the son of Jacob in the Old Testament, always had his dream fresh in his mind. His goals appeared as dreams. He kept talking of his dreams despite the opposition. Nothing could stop his rise. Frankly speaking, it is difficult to kill a man with a worthwhile vision or goal. Joseph refused to be distracted; Potiphar's wife came along, but Joseph's goal was in front of him. Let me take you through an exposition in Genesis 13:14 – 15,17

Genesis 13:14,15(NKJV)

And the LORD said to Abram, after Lot had separated from him: "Lift your eyes now and look from the place where you are — northward, southward, eastward, and westward; for all the land which you see I give to you and your descendants forever.

Lift your eyes now; now denotes that there is no place for procrastination. Why do you procrastinate on improving yourself? Why not do the study now? Why not pursue your purpose now? Why all the excuses? Don Wilder opines that 'excuses are the nails used to construct a house of failure'. Do not postpone what you can do now. You can do a master's degree or PhD now. Do not postpone it till you are married; this is just advice for someone reading this book.

The Lord said to Abraham, "What you see, you possess." If your goals can be before you, then there is a greater possibility of achieving them. At a point in school, I was informed that a student had all 'A's in his courses. So in my fourth year at the university as an electrical engineering student; I made it my goal to make all 'A's. I put the goal before me, prayed towards it, and even made a vow to God. And I got what I wanted. God should not take seriously what you are not serious about.

CHAPTER 7

WALKING IN DOMINION THROUGH WORSHIP

A child was on the airplane with his dad. While at a point in the air, the child peeped through the window and noticed some small-looking houses. He asked the dad if the inhabitants were as small as ants, because the houses were very small and he felt like a giant compared to the size of the houses. The dad had to explain that the houses were normal in size like theirs, but they were at a far greater height than the houses, hence the small looking appearance. Hence, nothing changed except their altitude. Altitude, as an online dictionary would put it, is 'the height of an object or point in relation to sea level or ground level.'

From inference, it can be said that if your problems appear too big, it is likely your altitude is too low. You need to step up your altitude. It really matters how you view things, talking about your perspective. We have a good example in Scripture; while others saw

Goliath as a giant, David saw him as something very small to deal with. David was operating from a higher altitude.

1 Samuel 17:32-33(TLB)

"Don't worry about a thing," David told him. "I'll take care of this Philistine!"

"Don't be ridiculous!" Saul replied. "How can a kid like you fight with a man like him? You are only a boy, and he has been in the army since he was a boy!"

The multitude saw Goliath as a BIG problem. Even King Saul could not understand the risk David was about to take. Yet, for David, Goliath was just a thing he would knock down and throw to the birds. A majority may be able to make a factual point, but that does not mean their decision is the best.

1 Samuel 17:46(CEV)

Today the Lord will help me defeat you. I'll knock you down and cut off your head, and I'll feed the bodies of the other Philistine soldiers to the birds and wild animals. Then the whole world will know that Israel has a real God.

Many times, our prayers are just complaints. We just spend time explaining to God how big your problems are; while we should be telling the problems how big our God is. Our altitude matters; when we are in the low plane, as being earthly, we see big problems. But perspective changes when we go to the heavenly levels. We have greater dominion from heavenly levels.

Ephesians 2:6 (TLB)
and lifted us up from the grave into glory along with Christ, ***where we sit with him in the heavenly realms****-all because of what Christ Jesus did.*

From the level God views things, all things are possible. So the Scripture says that '*with God all things are possible*' Matthew 19:26. When we enter his realm, and sit with him there, we begin to see as He sees. It is also written that as he is, so are we. Hence, at His level, all things also become possible for us.

Mark 9:23 (KJV)
Jesus said unto him, If thou canst believe, all things are possible to him that believeth.

The twelve spies sent by Moses into the land of Jericho were not on the same altitude or level. Hence, their perspectives were different. The spies looked at the same thing, but some people saw the adversaries as big as giants; another group saw them as small as a loaf of bread. The difference was in the altitudinal levels at which they were operating. Even the Almighty God acknowledged that Caleb had a different spirit and operated at a different level.

Numbers 13:31-33 (NKJV)

But the men who had gone up with him said, "We are not able to go up against the people, for they are stronger than we." And they gave the children of Israel a bad report of the land which they had spied out, saying, "The land through which we have gone as spies is a land that devours its inhabitants, and all the people whom we saw in it are men of great stature. There we saw the giants (the descendants of Anak came from the giants); and we were like grasshoppers in our own sight, and so we were in their sight."

Numbers 14:6-9 (NKJV)

But Joshua the son of Nun and Caleb the son of Jephunneh, who were among those who had spied out the land, tore their clothes; and they spoke to all the congregation of the children of Israel, saying: "The land we passed through to spy out is an exceedingly good land. If the Lord delights in us, then He will bring us into this land and give it to us, 'a land which flows with milk and honey.' Only do not rebel against the Lord, nor fear the people of the land, for they are our bread; their protection has departed from them, and the Lord is with us. Do not fear them."

Numbers 14:24 (NKJV)

But My servant Caleb, because he has a different spirit in him and has followed Me fully, I will bring into the land where he went, and his descendants shall inherit it.

These Scriptures make it clear that those who operate under fear cannot see in the same way that those who operate under faith can. Faith operates from a higher altitude. The higher your altitude, the smaller problems become. When you operate from the heavenlies where Christ is seated at the right hand of Authority, you have a high level of audacity.

Luke 1:19-20(NIV)

The angel answered, "I am Gabriel. I stand in the presence of God, and I have been sent to speak to you and to tell you this good news. And now you will be silent and not able to speak until the day this happens; because you did not believe my words, which will come true at their proper time."

You can feel the audacity with which Gabriel spoke because he dwells and stands in the presence of God. It would be easy to say that, as an angel, Gabriel was free to speak without fear; however, there was a man who was always in God's presence and was known for his audacity. That man was Elijah.

1 Kings 17:1(NKJV)

And Elijah the Tishbite, of the inhabitants of Gilead, said to Ahab,"As the Lord God of Israel lives, before whom I stand, there shall not be dew nor rain these years, except at my word."

1 Kings 18:15(NKJV)

Then Elijah said, "As the Lord of hosts lives, before whom I stand, I will surely present myself to him today."

When a man stands in God's presence and dwells at His courts, that man carries authority. It is written that he that dwells in the secret place of the Most

High shall abide under the shadow of the Almighty. That place (His courts) can be accessed through praise and sincere worship unto the Lord. When Paul and Silas worshipped God inside the prison with their songs of praise, the presence of the Lord had to come down, and the prison space could not contain the Almighty. The prison gates opened. Can you imagine God coming down to sit on the walls of Jericho when the children of Israel worshipped in obedience? The weight was too much for the walls, and you know what happened next. Dominion is manifested in an atmosphere of worship to the King of kings.

Psalms 8:2, 6(NKJV)

Out of the mouth of babes and nursing infants You have ordained strength, Because of Your enemies, That <u>You may silence the enemy and the avenger</u>.

You have made him <u>to have dominion</u> over the works of Your hands; You have put all things under his feet,

When Jesus quoted this verse, He said

Matthew 21:16 (NKJV)

... And Jesus said to them, "Yes. Have you never read, 'Out of the mouth of babes and nursing infants You have perfected praise'?"

When you praise God, you gain dominion and silence the enemies. Worship raises you to the level of His presence. Praise and worship embarrass the devil; when the devil believes he has you down and expects you to complain, and then praise and worship pour out, he has a heart attack. Let nothing steal your praise of God from your lips and heart.

ABOUT THE AUTHOR

Abinye Nwankwo is a multitalented person. A combination of great qualities from his late parents, Rev. Canon Israel A. Nwankwo and Dr. Mrs. Joyce N. Nwankwo has greatly influenced his lifestyle. He works diligently and carefully. He loves the Lord and wants the next generation to develop and uphold the faith. He is an entrepreneur who has aided many individuals in honing their abilities.

Engr Abinye Nwankwo earned a bachelor's degree in Electrical/Electronics Engineering before pursuing a master's degree in Electronics/Telecommunications. He also possessed a master's degree in Engineering Management. He is a member of Nigeria's Council for the Regulation of Engineering (COREN)

Uncle Abinye, as he is commonly known, has been inspiring talented children and teenagers for over twenty years. He is a gifted and inspirational writer who has written several influential books, including "Creating your season of Abundance," "The hurdle (fiction)," "Thy Kingdom come," "Strange things in Zion," "Ecclesiastical Epistles," "Train me – the yearning of every child," and others.

He is enthusiastic about teaching God's word. And he is always willing to learn more.

He is happily married to Dr. Mrs. Mercy Nwankwo, with whom he has five biological children (the E-series). Many other children look up to him and his wife as parents.

OTHER BOOKS BY THE AUTHOR

ECCLESIASTICAL EPISTLES

This book addresses some of the ills that plague the church of Christ today in a concise and easy-to-read manner. From dealing with pulpit exaggerations and the growing trend of substituting different items in place of the wonderful name of Jesus, to outright extortions. What could be the reason for so many people but less power in the church today? The author has shown bravery in bringing us back to Bible basics and reminding us of how Christian ministry should be.

All who are concerned about the future sanctity and relevance of the church must be aware of the content and intent of some messages from contemporary pulpits. This book will be enlightening and enriching for church leaders, workers, parents, and all lovers of God.

The book addresses some lies and flawed assumptions being released from the pulpit. Of course, it is well understood that if the foundation is poor, even the righteous will struggle. This book is jam-packed with great inspiration. Ecclesiastical epistles, indeed.

THE HURDLE (ìdíwọ)

In terms of challenges, each locality has its own peculiarities. Immorality and infidelity are prevalent in some communities, while some other communities have a high mortality rate. There was a time when children in northern Nigeria had a high rate of polio infection. When you think your situation is hopeless, you learn of a greater challenge somewhere else. Different families in the same neighbourhood may face different challenges. Men in some enclaves do not reach a certain age. In some families, girls give birth before marriage, while others have a specific disease trailing them. People give various reasons for the cause; some say it is environmental, while others say it is societal. Some will attribute it to coincidence, while others will claim it is spiritual.

This book is a FICTION and very intriguing, handling the issue of family trends.

CREATING YOUR SEASON OF ABUNDANCE

We have heard of countries experiencing seasons of famine and lack. It was in such a season and in such country that a man named Isaac was living in abundance. What happened? He created his season of abundance.

The basic principles for 'reproduction' affects both believers and non-believers. So also are financial principles. Yet many have refused to get knowledge on these principles. "My people", God said "are destroyed for lack of knowledge".

There is actually hope as this timely, down-to-earth and yet practical book teaches on matters relating to the following:

- Family Budgeting
- Savings and Investment
- Thrift and Cooperatives
- What destroys most FOREX traders
- Impulse buying- a form of financial leak

TRAIN ME - The yearning of every child

This manual focuses on the nurturing and instruction required to raise accountable and pious children. It imparts knowledge on family-related topics in an accessible format.

- Should a family hire domestic help?
- Should I use a cane to discipline my kids?
- Is keeping a family budget necessary?
- Why do children of strict parents lead rebellious lives?

These topics, as well as others, are covered in this book.

STRANGE THINGS IN ZION

Terrible things are happening in our churches and fellowships today, and of a kind that does not occur even among pagans. The fact that the world has become churchy does not permit us, the church to become worldly. Examine and purify yourselves beloved brethren in Christ. He that thinks he stands, should take heed lest he fall.

The fact that drama has become a major weapon of evangelism available to the Church today is not in doubt. It will however be fool hardy for us not to recognize the fact that the same weapon is equally useful to the kingdom of hell.

These pieces of drama put together by Abinye Nwankwo brings out the power of this weapon of evangelism. Today, many students on the campuses are terribly guilty of the issues raised in these pieces of drama. The messages are straightforward, direct and devoid of the unnecessary preambles that make the average Christian drama boring and dry.

It is a compilation of six Christian plays which could be acted as stage plays or adapted for drama productions.

www.ingramcontent.com/pod-product-compliance
Lightning Source LLC
LaVergne TN
LVHW091051150826
845673LV00002B/539

* 9 7 9 8 3 5 8 6 5 1 6 0 9 *